Naum Gabo

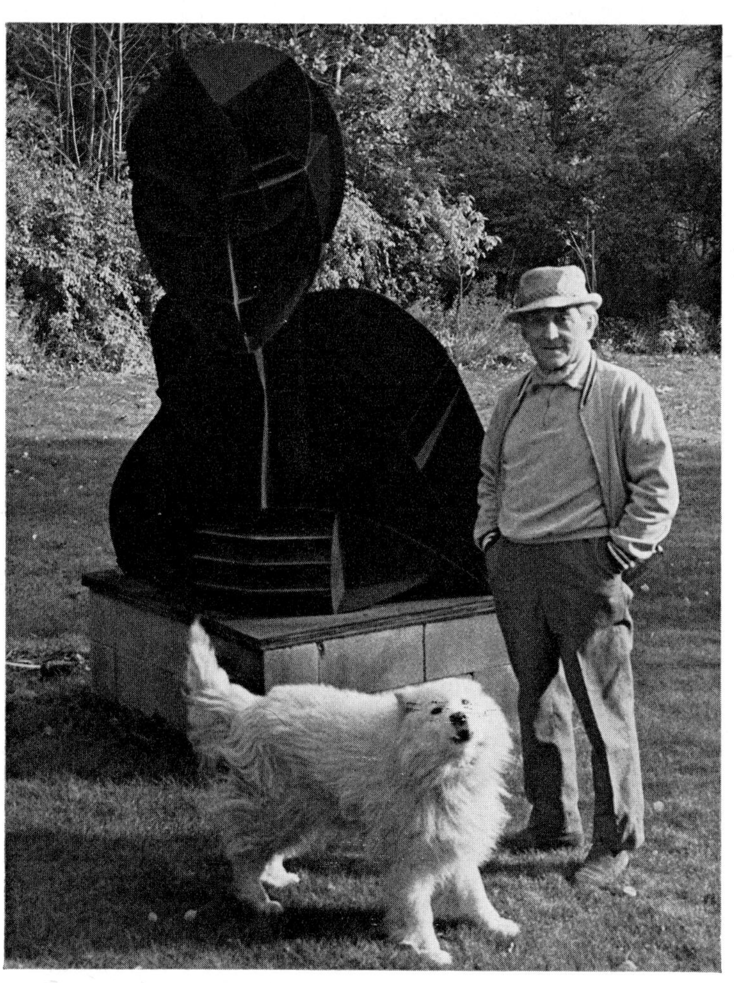

TERESA NEWMAN

NAUM GABO

THE CONSTRUCTIVE PROCESS

'Never look for any symbolic meanings in the images
of my work: there is no other meaning in them
than the images themselves'

Gabo, 1975

THE TATE GALLERY

Exclusively distributed in France and Italy by Idea Books
46–8 rue de Montreuil, 75011 Paris and Via Cappuccio 21, 20123 Milan

ISBN 0 905005 65 1
Published by order of the Trustees 1976
for the exhibition of 3 November–12 December 1976
Copyright © 1976 The Tate Gallery
Published by the Tate Gallery Publications Department,
Millbank, London SW1P 4RG
Designed by Pauline Key
Cover photograph by John Webb
Photography by Michael Duffett, David Nye
Blocks by Augustan Engravers Ltd. London
Printed in Great Britain by Balding & Mansell Ltd, Wisbech, Cambs.

Contents

Cover
Column (enlarged version 1975)
Catalogue No.19

Frontispiece
Gabo at Middlebury with his Samoyed 'Snieshka'
(Snowball), 1968

Foreword

Though small in size this exhibition contains a large number of the ideas and first drafts of a long lifetime's work. Naum Gabo is one of the most considerable artists of the twentieth century, but his sculptures have often had to wait many years before they could be realized on the scale he originally intended. The 'Head' of 1916 was not created in its final majestic form until 1956. In 1975 the discovery that suitable glass was now produced by Pilkingtons at last made it practicable to construct the large version of the 'Column' of 1923. The generosity of a private donor (Alistair McAlpine) and the enthusiasm of the architect Eugene Rosenberg meant that the delicate 'Torsion' of 1923 could grow into the nine-foot high fountain outside St. Thomas's Hospital.

As a privileged friend and an admirer of his work for many years I am delighted to be able to show Gabo's work at the Tate. Gabo has a particular affection for England and I think it is for this reason that he has allowed us to make this exhibition of the models; these are so close to his heart and to the inception of his ideas that they give a very special insight into his achievement.

Most of the works belong to the artist or to his family and I should like to take the opportunity to thank them, and also the several private collectors who have made this exhibition possible.

Norman Reid Director

Naum Gabo

The images of classic art are in one sense timeless. In another sense, they are always and uniquely products of a particular era of time, inspired by contemporary ideas in science and philosophy and giving expression to society's deepest aspirations. Out of the old equation of truth with beauty (or the *fact* of intellectual with the *hope* of moral progress), the classic artist creates symbolic and didactic images of an ordered universe where continuity, harmony and reason dispel chaos.

These intellectual and symbolic qualities are abundantly present in Gabo's oeuvre born as it is not only of twentieth-century science and philosophy but of the Russian Revolution with the utopian hopes it engendered and which, in one way or another, have affected so many subsequent movements in art. What is unique about Gabo is that events have destroyed neither his curiosity nor his optimism.

Although Gabo was well aware of contemporary ideas in art during his years at Munich University (1910–14), he never trained as an artist but came to sculpture as a result of his studies in engineering and physics. While the discoveries of Einstein and other physicists concerning the complex structure of the universe, the dematerialization of matter, and the space/time continuum were already being absorbed in European intellectual and artistic circles before the war, Gabo was the first artist fully to grasp the implications of these ideas, in particular for sculpture with its age-old tradition of the mono-lithic mass. Already by 1914 he was searching for a way to translate the new poetry of space and time into valid sculptural images and, finding nothing in contemporary art to satisfy his vision, it was to modern engineering techniques and modern industrial materials that he turned, as he has continued to do, for a means.

The other aspect of Gabo's art, its utopianism, was crystallized in the immediate aftermath of the Revolution when Gabo, who had returned to Russia via Norway in 1917, experienced a unique, brief, but never to be forgotten opportunity to provide active cultural leadership for the masses. In the new revolutionary State the need for a revolutionary art seemed pressing, and out of the ferment of arguments and ideas generated at the time, Gabo defined his own Constructive aesthetic in the *Realistic Manifesto*, pasted on the Moscow hoardings in August, 1920. The position he adopted, within the ideological quarrels of the time, was substantially that of Malevich in his uncompromising commitment to art as an independent, spiritual activity, and rejection of Tatlin's anti-art, functionalist ideas.

Nevertheless, even at that time, Gabo's aesthetic emerged as quite distinct from that of Malevich. Constructivism was and is 'real' in the sense that it consists of three-dimensional, palpable images set in space and addressed to a wide audience. But constructive reality also has a philosophical dimension insofar as these sensuous images express a modern, life-affirming consciousness with materials and methods appropriate to our time. The constructive principle, in Gabo's words, 'embraces the whole complex of human relationships to life: it is a mode of thinking, acting, perceiving and living'.[1] Creation, for Gabo, is another word for life.

To place his art in a broader historical perspective, Gabo later redefined his position in terms of a much older Russian tradition which he has characterized as 'idealistic in its spiritual function, utilitarian in its social function, and abstract in its formal content'.[2] But to the aesthetic and moral imperatives of the *Realistic Manifesto* Gabo has consistently held, as a consideration of his development over sixty years must confirm.

10

Most previous exhibitions of Gabo's work have concentrated upon completed constructions. This small exhibition, by contrast, focuses on the many preparatory studies—drawings, paintings and models —by which Gabo has over a sixty year period brought his ideas to fruition. These works not only form an important, and hitherto somewhat neglected corpus in Gabo's work, but they remind us that his art has been in a continuous state of evolution, of 'moving towards' an ideal which, once realized, has in turn been superseded. For whilst each individual work makes an authoritative statement, the Constructive philosophy sees none as necessarily 'complete' but open, like life itself, to further growth and development. Gabo's is a deeply meditated art, characterized by the patient, systematic and ingenious way by which he has developed a few central preoccupations into sculptural images of ever greater effectiveness. From the small sketches made in 1917 to the complex structures of his maturity, Gabo's oeuvre illustrates his own maxim: 'Great works of art are not made in a day, nor some in a year.'

'All my drawings', Gabo has said, 'contain the seeds of an idea or an image which may be developed in a sculpture'.[3] In fact, these sketches and drawings in which Gabo sets down his first ideas for a project show him at his most spontaneous and provide many valuable insights into his intentions. Some—for example the sketch for 'Spheric Theme'—have a 'visionary' character which could not be deduced from the resulting construction. Certain drawings and watercolours are clearly isolated experiments, either suggestions for possible future development, or ways of exploring kinetic ideas in two dimensions but, in the majority of drawings shown here, the relationship to a finished construction is clear enough. In some of the early drawings, their destination as constructions in space can be inferred from the large area of empty paper surrounding the small pencilled image.

The interval between sketch or drawing and the small three-dimensional working model into which it is translated varies.

Sometimes it seems to have been rapid, but in certain cases, particularly before 1925, there was a longer 'gestation' period. For instance, the projects for an institute of physics and mathematics and for an airport, mooted in sketches as early as 1919 were not realized in three dimensions before the mid-twenties and other ideas such as 'Spheric Theme' seem to have taken many months to materialize. Some of these tiny models, which Gabo has always made and which exist for all his constructions, are, like the drawings, experimental 'notes'; most, however, are remarkable for the completeness with which they establish the image–the appearance, character and proportions–of each final work, requiring only to be enlarged to the scale envisaged. All the models before 1950 are made of plastics and the most obvious modification therefore has been in terms of materials, although these too are usually envisaged from the outset. In certain early works, for example 'Column' of 1923, glass and metal were better able to serve the transparency, rigidity and luminosity of the theme, but increasingly, as Gabo's ideas developed, improvements in the transparency and strength of industrial plastics rendered such modifications unnecessary, as a comparison of most models from the mid-1920s (eg 'Construction in Space ''2 Cones''') with the finished work shows. Those made for some later, technically very complex structures (for example at the Bijenkorf, Rotterdam, 1954–7) appear as very simplified prototypes, but even these accurately establish the general aesthetic character of the work.

Most of Gabo's models were enlarged to full–if not always final –scale in a single operation, but in a few cases there are 'intermediate' versions, some of which are shown here within their evolving context.

In the works of the post-war period the procedures become more complicated. Although Gabo continued, as the works shown here confirm, to make drawings and models for all his constructions, their growing numbers, richness, scale and complexity, and the rapidity with which each work generated its successor, blurs any distinction between 'preparation' and realization. Each completed work becomes a stage in the constructive process, some being absorbed into larger structures, others being used as elements in compositions involving several structures. A new monumentality accompanies this trend and from the 1950s Gabo enlarged a number of earlier constructions, often using new materials and slightly altering the form to give them new dimensions of meaning. Examples of such enlargements shown here are 'Head No.2', of 1916, 'Column', of 1923, 'Torsion', 1929 and 'Spheric Theme' 1935–7, all remade within the last fifteen years.

Just as any discussion of Gabo's art must take account of the philosophy of Constructivism, so the question of scale in Gabo's work cannot be considered except in the context of his lifelong ambition to make a 'public' art. This was explicit, both in the *Realistic Manifesto*, and in the open-air exhibition on Tverskoi Boulevard which it accompanied: 'On the squares and in the streets we are placing our works, convinced that art must not remain a sanctuary for the idle, a consolation for the rich . . . Art should attend us everywhere that life flows and acts . . .'. Despite the frustration of Gabo's hopes, for much of his working life, by the massive indifference of our century to monumental art, Gabo has never relinquished his early vision and his works have been described, accurately, as so many blueprints for a public art.[4]

In the heroic period following the Revolution (1917–22) Gabo, like many fellow artists, designed a number of public projects, a series of architecturally inspired monuments and towers whose function was to commemorate the technological achievements of the new society and symbolize its aspirations (of these projects the most famous is Tatlin's 'Monument to the Third International'). Gabo's own ideas at this time included sketches for a radio station, for a physics observatory and two projects shown here, 'Model for Monument for an Airport' and 'Sketch for a Monument for an Institute of Physics and Mathematics'.

All Gabo's early drawings and many later ones, no matter how small, show him continually aspiring to the condition of architecture. After his move to Berlin in 1922, these preoccupations at first continued. In 'Column', 1923, Gabo resolved his search for an image which would fuse the architectural with the sculptural, but he was not able to enlarge it to its present monumental scale for over fifty years. If patronage in post-revolutionary Russia had been uncertain and capricious, in Berlin at this date it seems to have been almost non-existent, and the evident shift in Gabo's work away from 'architectonic' towards an 'object' mode after 1924 must reflect this reality.

During his time in Berlin, Gabo received only one public commission, from the City Architect, to design a scheme for a 'Fête Lumière' (1929). The project never materialized and survives only in the photograph exhibited here, but it is possible to recapture some of the excitement of Gabo's 'Russian' period in the notion of projecting vast patterns of electric light rays onto the night sky from specially designed wooden bases. What better way to express the excitement of technological progress and symbolize the aspirations of a modern city; one can imagine this was a project after Gabo's heart. One other important commission, but destined for a more restricted audience, came from Diaghilev in 1926, to design the set and costumes for the one-act ballet *La Chatte* choreographed by Georges Balanchine. In accepting this commission, Gabo became one of a long line of Russian artists who designed for the ballet and one of many, including Benois and Bakst, who worked for Diaghilev. His Constructivist set, designed to revolve in harmony with the dancers' movements, is among the most abstract and radical of any designed for the Ballets Russes. The set forms, too, an important milestone in Gabo's own art, since he was for the first time able to realize a complex kinetic construction on a large scale.

In 1946, after eleven fruitful years in England, Gabo settled in the United States. When at last he received and was able to carry out his first public commission, for a construction at the Baltimore Museum of Art (see photograph and model for the lower section of this) his delight was apparent: 'There is nothing more satisfactory for an artist than to see his work in a public place, especially for the first time . . . Although I have designed many monumental works this is the first I have been given the opportunity to execute. I find myself in a state of increased vitality – which I have not experienced before'.[5] To this state of increased vitality, and the stimulus of other commissions, one may attribute the new blossoming of Gabo's art from that time. Although the Esso Building project failed to materialize, there were compensations in the commission (1956) to design a structure for the U.S. Rubber Company Building, in winning 2nd prize in the international competition for a 'Monument to the Unknown Political Prisoner' (1953) and in the important commission (1954) to erect a construction, 80ft high, at the Bijenkorf, Rotterdam. In these and other late works Gabo's art achieved the monumental status, and the public, it had always sought.

'Space and time are the only forms upon which life is built and hence art must be constructed.' Of the twin poles on which the *Realistic Manifesto* was launched the preoccupation with space has been perhaps the most obvious feature of Gabo's art. In terms specific to sculpture, Gabo renounced 'volume and mass as plastic forms of space', substituting instead the concept of space as continuous depth and abolishing with it the 'descriptive' lines of the past. 'We affirm the line only as a direction of static forces (of things) and their rhythms in objects'. So far as his own experiments in spatial construction were concerned, Gabo could speak with some confidence since he had already, before coming back to Russia, perfected a system of stereometric construction; adapted from engineering practice, in a series of Heads, of which the small iron 'Head No.2' of 1916 is a surviving example. Based on the theoretical principle of infinite expansion from a central core, these structures, made of wood, celluloid or metal, comprised the intersection of two or more planes, to which were added a large number of subsidiary planes, each carefully shaped, glued or welded together and placed at right angles to the ostensible 'skin' or surface of the image. The interior was thus revealed as a series of open volumes. This fresh and economical solution to an artistic problem is simply demonstrated by a comparison of Gabo's two cubes, one closed, the other 'stereometric' and open. But, as the resulting choice of a human image shows, Gabo's aim was primarily one of more effective *communication* 'What was it I tried to do in these constructions? . . . I transferred myself to the middle of the construction, to be in the middle of space so to speak. Space is in me, it comes out of me. There are ways in which the artist can make the spectator feel that he, the spectator, is within the sculpture'.[6]

Gabo's ways consisted, first, in the creation of structures themselves open to the enveloping space, next in making these structures transparent, implying immateriality, and finally in suggesting their hidden rhythms or energy by the use of spiralling directional lines (as will be made clear, Gabo's use of 'lines of force', although related to that of the Futurists, had little real connection with their ideas.) All these factors can be seen in the transparent 'Column', with its circular base and lateral curving elements. Shortly afterwards, Gabo began to abandon this 'angular' conception of space in favour, increasingly, of a curved one, seeking a poetic analogy perhaps for the ideas of Einstein and other physicists in this respect. Examples of this mode of the mid-twenties are 'Circular Relief', of 1925, and 'Construction in Space ''2 Cones''' 1927. This growing search for a more satisfying image of space culminated in the invention, around 1935, of the 'Spheric Theme', which encloses space within a continuously curving surface, an image also of continuity which formed the basis of many later constructions. Simultaneously, Gabo's preoccupation with transparency increased, and perhaps the most beautiful and successful work of the 1920s is his plastic 'Torsion' (1929), a synthesis of spiralling transparent structure with space itself.

In the crystalline constructions of the later thirties, Gabo's preoccupation with transparency as a means of suggesting essences and the void assumed neo-platonic proportions, as his own description of them would seem to confirm: 'Transparent materials give me the chance to dematerialize as much as possible the content of my work of art. By dematerialization I mean to make it as near as possible to a spiritual object'. These constructions are, formally speaking, marvellously concentrated images in which shape, space and line are fused to poetic effect—and in which, incidentally, the last remaining vestiges of scientific 'apparatus' are shed. In the pursuit of such images Gabo used, or proposed to use, not only space itself but translucent plastics whose forms were 'defined' by their light-emitting edges, rays of sun or electric light, crystals, water, light-conducting lines delicately incised upon transparent surfaces, and pure white nylon threads. By increasingly ingenious and inspired use of these substances Gabo developed his space-frame constructions, a process one can follow stage by stage from the 'Construction on a Plane', through a succession of space 'envelopes' to the stringed 'Linear Construction No.1' of 1942–3. In the latter work the only 'solid' element is the square perspex frame upon which Gabo, to establish a notional 'surface', stretched a complex array of luminous strings around an elliptical void.

Along with this increasingly complex play of *lines*, one observes greater emphasis from the later thirties on organic and fluid *shapes*, a development which may have been accelerated by Gabo's experience of stone carving and his consideration of organic form. 'Stone' shapes are also treated in many drawings. Echoes of his 'spiralling' stones can be seen both in the perspex 'Spiral Theme' (1941) and in another masterpiece 'Linear Construction No.2' of 1949–53, an airy and ethereal image which, in its suspended form, further enhanced

Gabo's poetry of space with actual motion. From this it was only a step to the introduction of the motorized kinetic structures and with these a new emphasis on the fourth dimension—Time.

The idea of kinetic art was first proposed by the Futurists and certain of Balla's sculptures come very close to actual movement, but the *Realistic Manifesto*, while acknowledging this source, rejects with uncompromising disdain the Futurists' 'provincial' equation of movement with speed and noise of modern life. 'Look at a ray of sun . . . the stillest of the still forces, it speeds more than 300 kilometres a second . . . behold our starry firmament . . . who hears it? What are our earthly trains to those hurrying trains of the galaxies?' Gabo's own 'Kinetic Construction, (Standing Wave)' of 1920 was (probably) the first motorized sculpture, but in the same fastidious and exacting spirit Gabo rejected it as *art*, on the grounds that its mechanism was as yet too rudimentary for the silent image he wanted to convey. It was not until 1975, over half a century later, that Gabo saw what is essentially the same idea (the transcribing of spiralling volumes through space) realized in the 'Torsion Fountain' at St. Thomas's Hospital.

In fact, much of Gabo's earlier work, being concerned with the concept of energy, does convey a sensation of dynamic movement (not speed), but just as we have seen space given a new spiritual and poetic dimension in the works of the later 1930s, so around that time the primary sensation of motion begins to give way to one of time. Time, as well as movement, seems implicit in such images as 'Torsion', with its suggestion of growth, in the carving of stones—natural products of time—with radial lines traced by a moving chisel, in such images of continuity as the 'Spheric Theme' and in the 'repetitive' stringing of the linear constructions. To experience these works is to become conscious of the duration of time. As an alternative to the use of lines, in certain later works (eg the Bijenkorf construction) the time element is brought into the spectator's consciousness by his own movement around the construction which presents him with a continuously changing image, such changes becoming an integral part of his experience of the work's existence in time. This idea was implicit already in the 1916 'Head', but became more pronounced in the later works. Here, for instance, is Reyner Banham's account of the Baltimore piece, a 15ft high construction suspended into the stair well of the Baltimore Art Centre: 'Looking up from the foot of the stairs the moving spectator sees the construction of metals and plastics as a single, complex, but apparently compact system of inter-laces. As he approaches it up the stairs it gradually separates out into two independent structures, one on the ceiling, the other below it, and when he achieves the upper landing, the separation becomes complete, the lower component [seen here in the model] hanging mostly slightly below the spectator's eye level, so that the sequence of viewpoints has passed from pure plan to pure elevation'.[7]

More commonly, however, in his later works, Gabo has drawn attention to the time factor by the use of motorized components. Their aesthetic and philosophical implications are enhanced as the slowly revolving image is continuously reversed under the changing play of light, the movement evoking a cycle of transformation and rebirth, a dance to the music of time. The spectator's experience of a work is enhanced as time is made palpable, to induce such involvement being the whole purpose and justification of Constructivist art. Gabo's mastery of time also has much to do with our recognition that he is one of the rare classic artists of the twentieth century, whose images have the power radically to extend our consciousness of reality. In a sense this small exhibition too is a meditation on time, since we are at once conscious of the passing of many years and of Gabo's synoptic unity of vision which may be apprehended in a moment.

NOTES

[1] Constructive Art: an exchange of letters between Naum Gabo and Sir Herbert Read, *Horizon*, July 1944; reprinted in *Gabo*, Lund Humphries, 1957.
[2] *Of Divers Arts*, V, p.131.
[3] Letter of 30 August 1976 to compiler.
[4] David Thompson, 'Outlines for a Public Art', *Studio International*, April 1966.
[5] Speech made at the installation ceremony, reprinted in *Baltimore Museum Bulletin*, November 1951.
[6] 'Naum Gabo talks about his work', *Studio International*, April 1966.
[7] *Architectural Review*, March 1955.

The Realistic Manifesto, 1920

Above the tempests of our weekdays,

Across the ashes and cindered homes of the past,

Before the gates of the vacant future,

We proclaim today to you artists, painters, sculptors, musicians, actors, poets . . . to you people to whom Art is no mere ground for conversation but the source of real exaltation, our word and deed.

The impasse into which Art has come to in the last twenty years must be broken.

The growth of human knowledge with its powerful penetration into the mysterious laws of the world which started at the dawn of this century,

The blossoming of a new culture and a new civilization with their unprecedented-in-history surge of the masses towards the possession of the riches of Nature, a surge which binds the people into one union, and last, not least, the war and the revolution (those purifying torrents of the coming epoch), have made us face the fact of new forms of life, already born and active.

What does Art carry into this unfolding epoch of human history?

Does it possess the means necessary for the construction of the new Great Style?

Or does it suppose that the new epoch may not have a new style?

Or does it suppose that the new life can accept a new creation which is constructed on the foundations of the old?

In spite of the demand of the renascent spirit of our time, Art is still nourished by impression, external appearance, and wanders helplessly back and forth from Naturalism to Symbolism, from Romanticism to Mysticism.

The attempts of the Cubists and the Futurists to lift the visual arts from the bogs of the past have led only to new delusions.

Cubism, having started with simplification of the representative technique ended with its analysis and stuck there.

The distracted world of the Cubists, broken in shreds by their logical anarchy, cannot satisfy us who have already accomplished the Revolution or who are already constructing and building up anew.

One could heed with interest the experiments of the Cubists, but one cannot follow them, being convinced that their experiments are being made on the surface of Art and do not touch on the bases of it seeing plainly that the end result amounts to the same old graphic, to the same old volume and to the same decorative surface as of old.

One could have hailed Futurism in its time for the refreshing sweep of its announced Revolution in Art, for its devastating criticism of the past, as in no other way could one have assailed those artistic barricades of 'good taste' . . . powder was needed for that and a lot of it . . . but one cannot construct a system of art on one revolutionary phrase alone.

One had to examine Futurism beneath its appearance to realize that one faced a very ordinary chatterer, a very agile and prevaricating guy, clad in the tatters of worn-out words like 'patriotism', 'militarism', 'contempt for the female', and all the rest of such provincial tags.

In the domain of purely pictorial problems, Futurism has not gone further than the renovated effort to fix on the canvas a purely optical reflex which has already shown its bankruptcy with the Impressionists. It is obvious now to every one of us that by the simple graphic registration of a row of momentarily arrested movements, one cannot re-create movement itself. It makes one think of the pulse of a dead body.

The pompous slogan of 'Speed' was played from the hands of the Futurists as a great trump. We concede the sonority of that slogan and we quite see how it can sweep the strongest of the provincials off their feet. But ask any Futurist how does he imagine 'speed' and there will emerge a whole arsenal of frenzied automobiles, rattling railway depots, snarled wires, the clank and the noise and the clang of carouselling streets . . . does one really need to convince them that all that is not necessary for speed and for its rhythms?

Look at a ray of sun . . . the stillest of the still forces, it speeds more than 300 kilometres in a second . . . behold our starry firmament . . . who hears it . . . and yet what are our depots to those depots of the Universe? What are our earthly trains to those hurrying trains of the galaxies?

Indeed, the whole Futurist noise about speed is too obvious an anecdote, and from the moment that Futurism proclaimed that 'Space and Time are yesterday's dead', it sunk into the obscurity of abstractions.

Neither Futurism nor Cubism has brought us what our time has expected of them.

Besides those two artistic schools our recent past has had nothing of importance or deserving attention.

But Life does not wait and the growth of generations does not stop and we who go to relieve those who have passed into history, having in our hands the results of their experiments, with their mistakes and their achievements, after years of experience equal to centuries . . . we say . . .

No new artistic system will withstand the pressure of a growing new culture until the very foundation of Art will be erected on the real laws of Life.

Until all artists will say with us . . .

All is a fiction . . . only life and its laws are authentic and in life only the active is beautiful and wise and strong and right, for life does not know beauty as an aesthetic measure . . . efficacious existence is the highest beauty.

Life knows neither good nor bad nor justice as a measure of morals . . . need is the highest and most just of all morals.

Life does not know rationally abstracted truths as a measure of cognizance, deed is the highest and surest of truths.

Those are the laws of life. Can art withstand these laws if it is built on abstraction, on mirage, and fiction?

We say . . .

Space and time are re-born to us today.

Space and time are the only forms on which life is built and hence art must be constructed.

States, political and economic systems perish, ideas crumble, under the strain of ages . . . but life is strong and grows and time goes on in its real continuity.

Who will show us forms more efficacious than this . . . who is the great one who will give us foundations stronger than this?

Who is the genius who will tell us a legend more ravishing than this prosaic tale which is called life?

The realization of our perceptions of the world in the forms of space and time is the only aim of our pictorial and plastic art.

In them we do not measure our works with the yardstick of beauty, we do not weigh them with pounds of tenderness and sentiments.

The plumb-line in our hand, eyes as precise as a ruler, in a spirit as taut as a compass . . . we construct our work as the universe constructs its own, as the engineer constructs his bridges, as the mathematician his formula of the orbits.

We know that everything has its own essential image; chair, table, lamp, telephone, book, house, man . . . they are all entire worlds with their own rhythms, their own orbits.

That is why we in creating things take away from them the labels of their owners . . . all accidental and local, leaving only the reality of the constant rhythm of the forces in them.

1. Thence in painting we renounce colour as a pictorial element, colour is the idealized optical surface of objects; an exterior and superficial impression of them; colour is accidental and it has nothing in common with the innermost essence of a thing.

We affirm *that the tone of a substance, i.e. its light-absorbing material body is its only pictorial reality.*

2. We renounce *in a line, its descriptive value; in real life there are no descriptive lines, description is an accidental trace of a man on things, it is not bound up with the essential life and constant structure of the body. Descriptiveness is an element of graphic illustration and decoration.*

We affirm *the line only as a direction of the static forces and their rhythm in objects.*

3. We renounce *volume as a pictorial and plastic form of space; one cannot measure space in volumes as one cannot measure liquid in yards: look at our space . . . what is it if not one continuous depth?*

We affirm *depth as the only pictorial and plastic form of space.*

4. We renounce *in sculpture, the mass as a sculptural element.*

It is known to every engineer that the static forces of a solid body and its material strength do not depend on the quantity of the mass . . . example a rail, a T-beam etc.

But you sculptors of all shades and directions, you still adhere to the age-old prejudice that you cannot free the volume of mass. Here (in this exhibition) we take four planes and we construct with them the same volume as of four tons of mass.

Thus we bring back to sculpture the line as a direction and in it we affirm depth as the one form of space.

5. We renounce *the thousand-year-old delusion in art that held the static rhythms as the only elements of the plastic and pictorial arts.*

We affirm *in these arts a new element the kinetic rhythms as the basic forms of our perception of real time.*

These are the five fundamental principles of our work and our constructive technique.

Today we proclaim our words to you people. In the squares and on the streets we are placing our work convinced that art must not remain a sanctuary for the idle, a consolation for the weary, and a justification for the lazy. Art should attend us everywhere that life flows and acts . . . at the bench, at the table, at work, at rest, at play; on working days and holidays . . . at home and on the road . . . in order that the flame to live should not extinguish in mankind.

We do not look for justification, neither in the past nor in the future.

Nobody can tell us what the future is and what utensils does one eat it with.

Not to lie about the future is impossible and one can lie about it at will.

We assert that the shouts about the future are for us the same as the tears about the past: a renovated day-dream of the romantics.

A monkish delirium of the heavenly kingdom of the old attired in contemporary clothes.

He who is busy today with the morrow is busy doing nothing.

And he who tomorrow will bring us nothing of what he has done today is of no use for the future.

Today is the deed.

We will account for it tomorrow.

The past we are leaving behind as carrion.

The future we leave to the fortune-tellers.

We take the present day.

NAUM GABO
ANTOINE PEVSNER
2nd State Printing House

Moscow, 5 August 1920

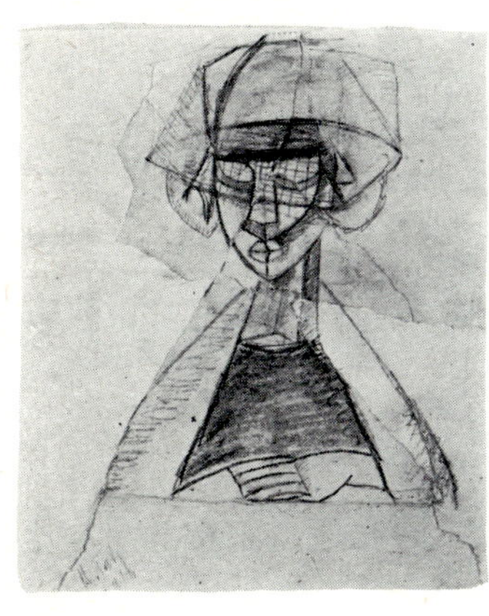

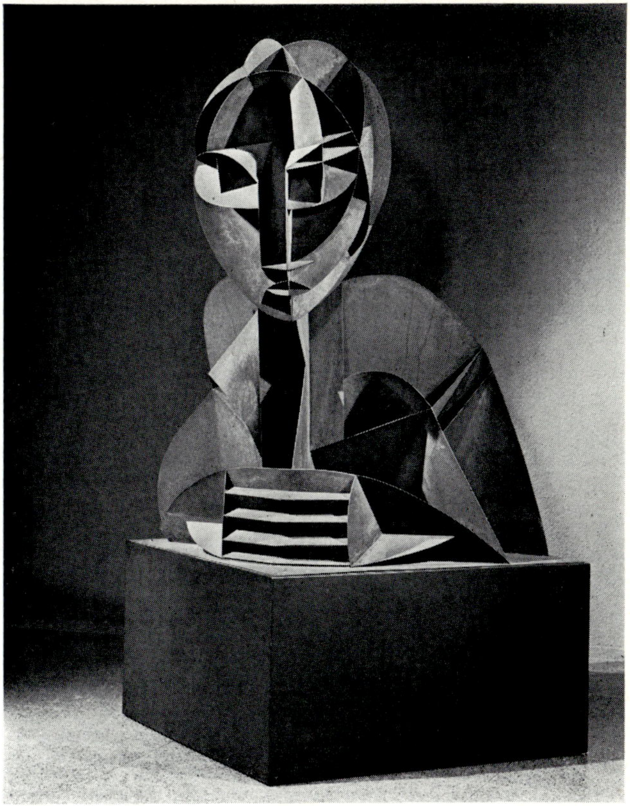

Above
3 Drawing for a constructed head 1916

Right
1 Head No.2
(enlarged version 1964)

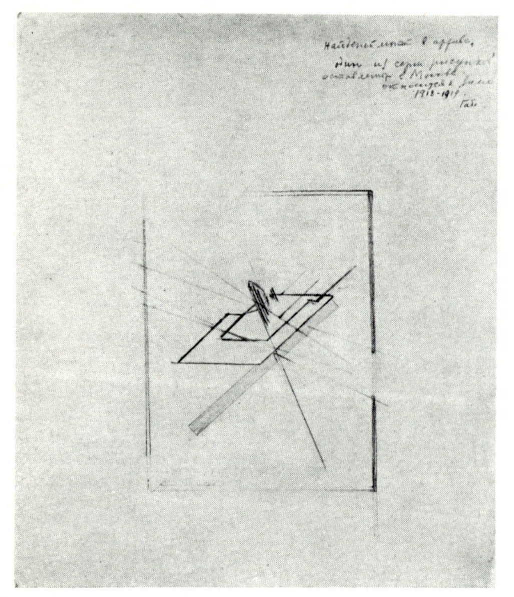

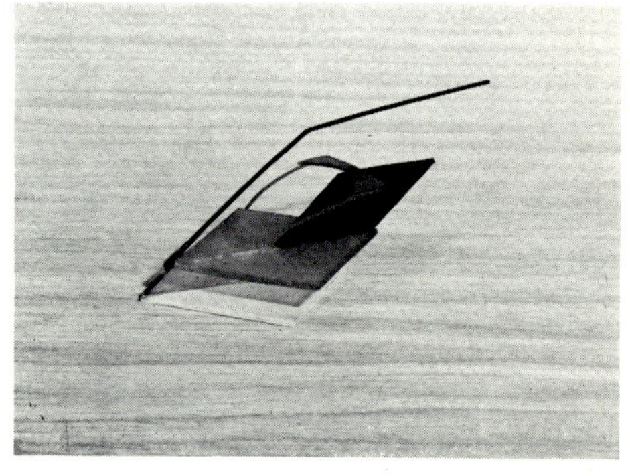

Left
20 Sketch 1918–19

Above
**21 Model for Monument
for an Airport** 1932

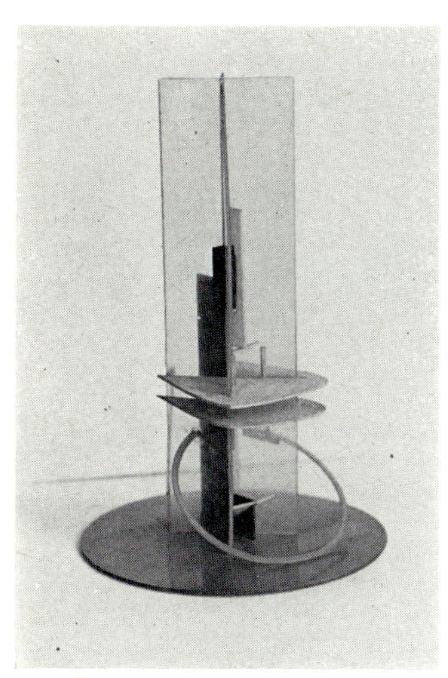

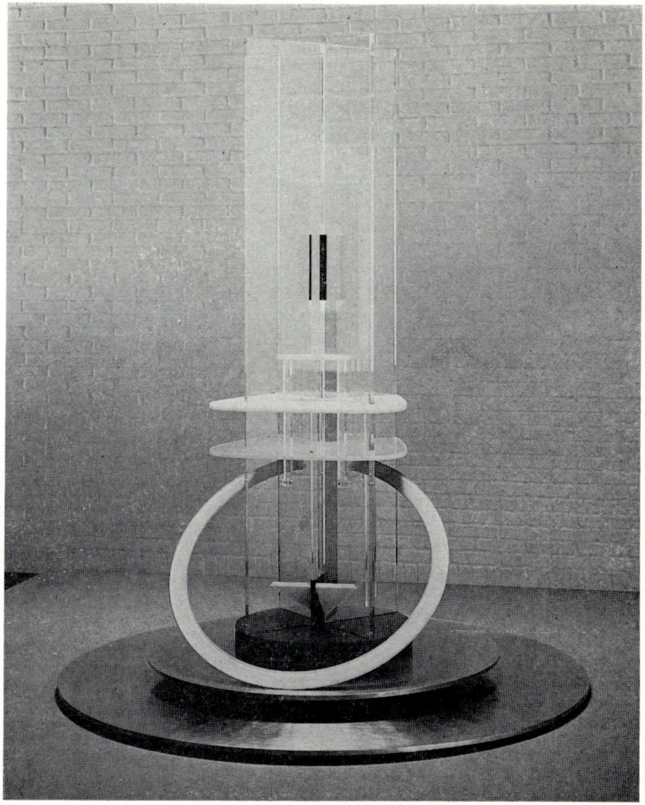

Above
17 Model for 'Column' 1923

Right
19 Column
(enlarged version 1975)

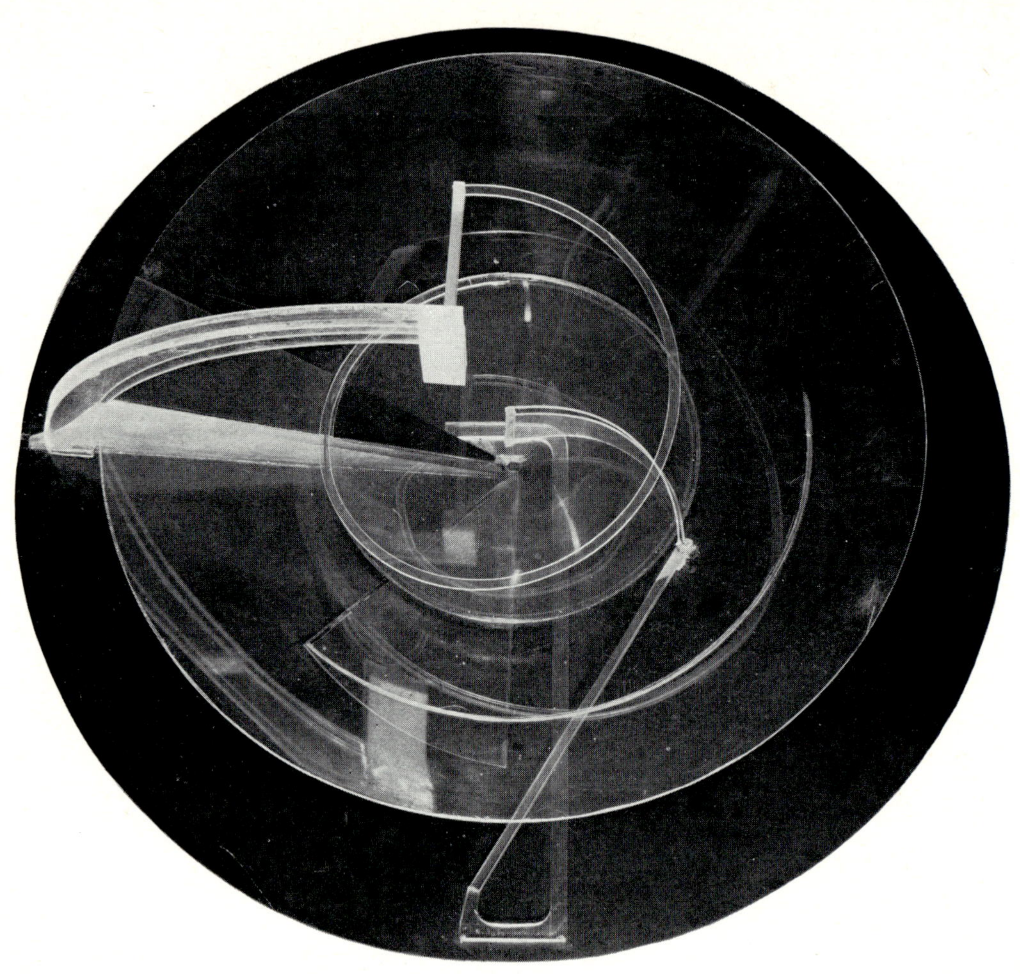

Left
22 Circular Relief 1925

Right
23 Model for 'Construction in Space
"2 Cones"' 1927

Below
25 Model for 'Double Relief in a Niche' c.1929

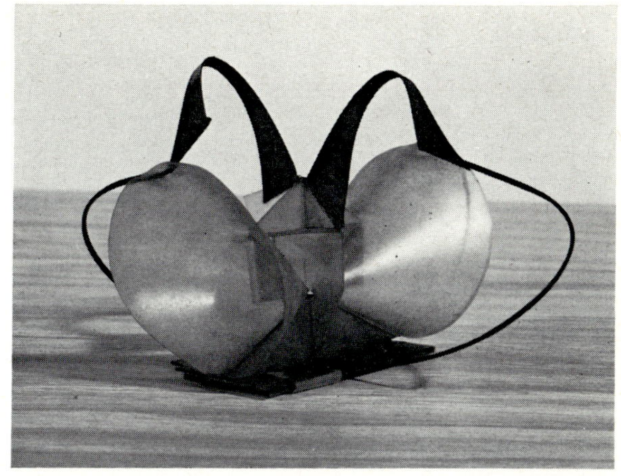

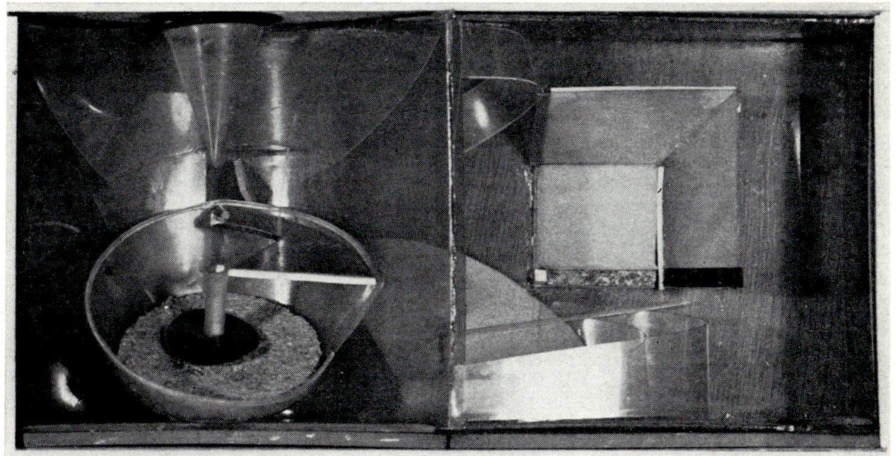

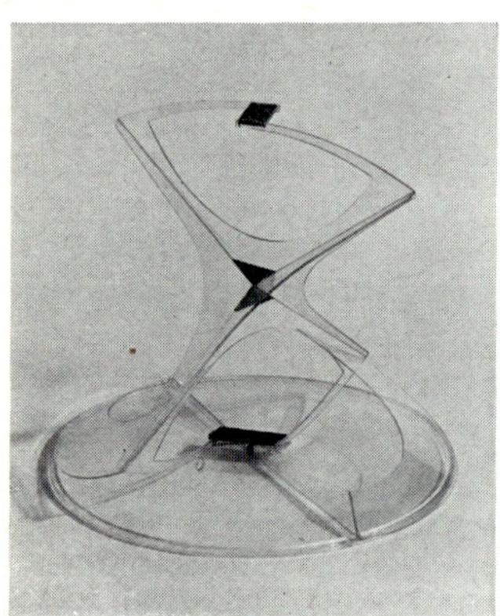

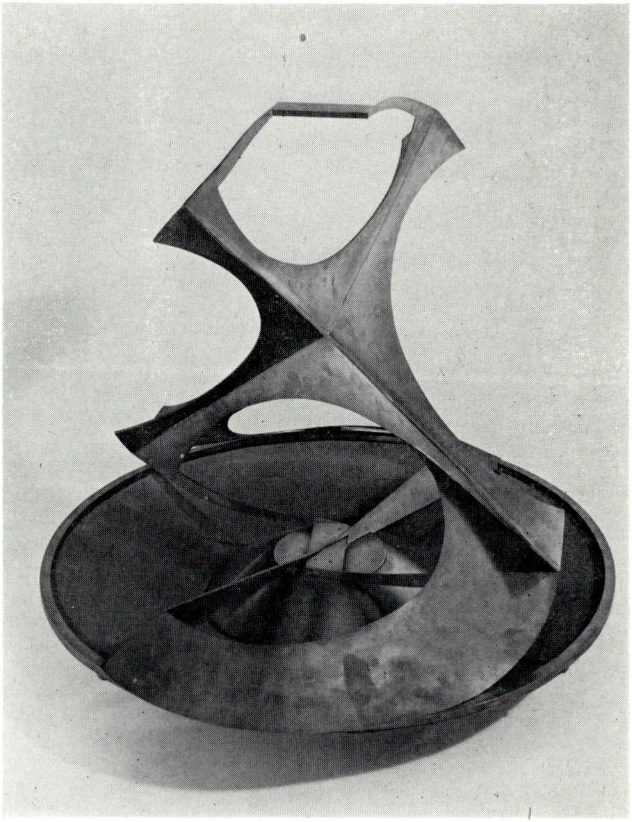

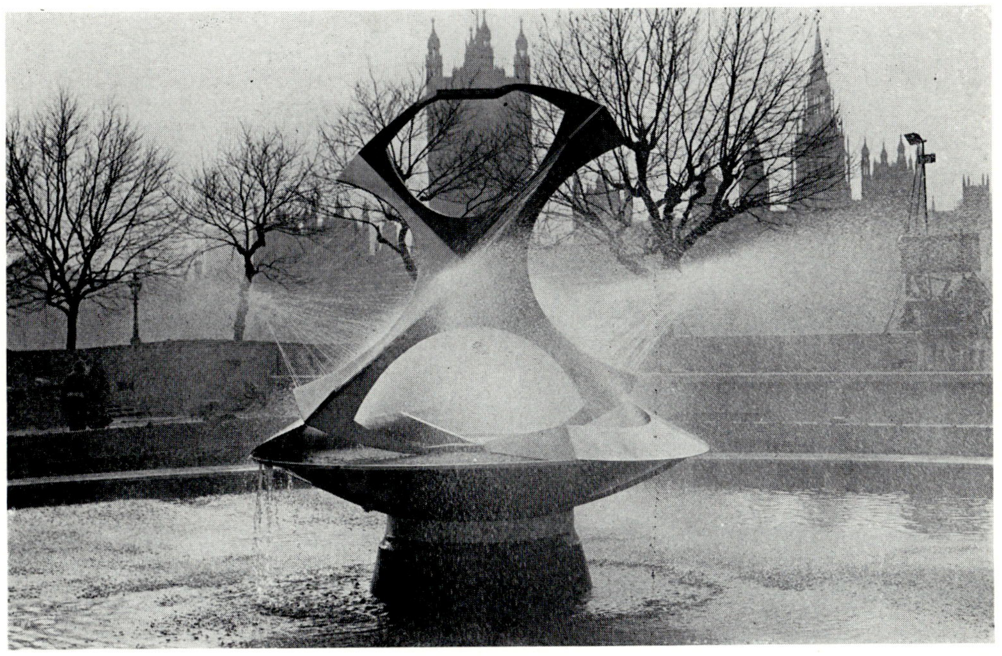

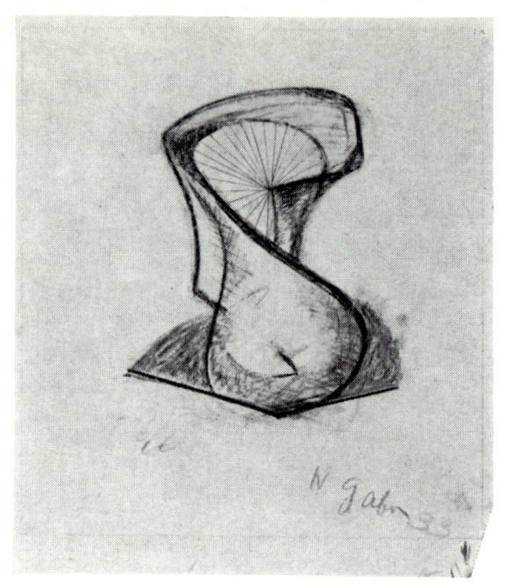

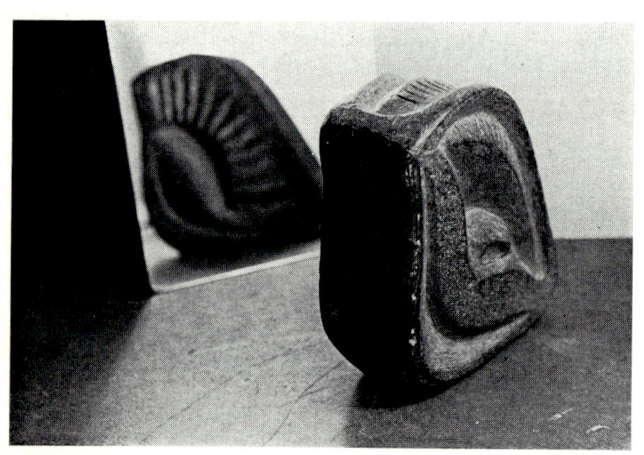

Above
39 Sketch for a stone carving 1933

Left
47 Granite Carving c.1940

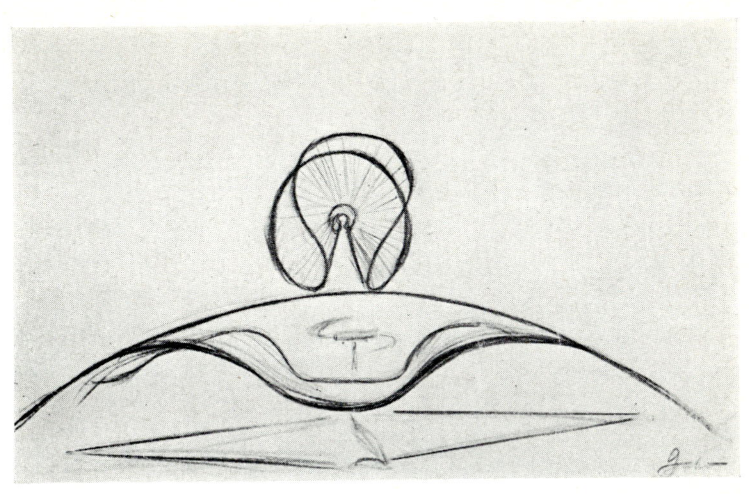

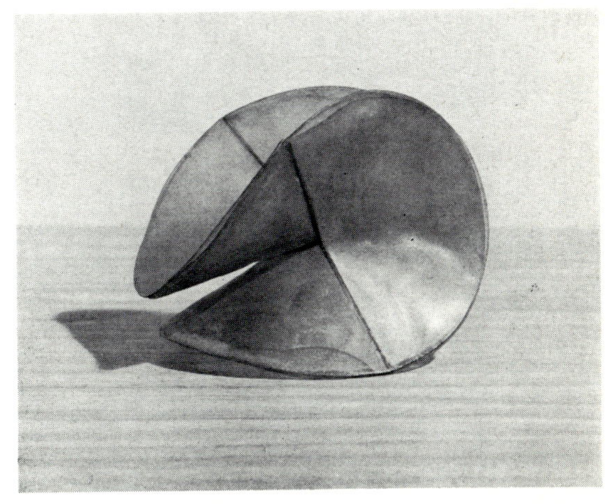

Above
48 Sketch for 'Spheric Theme' 1935–7

Right
50 Model for 'Spheric Theme' c.1937

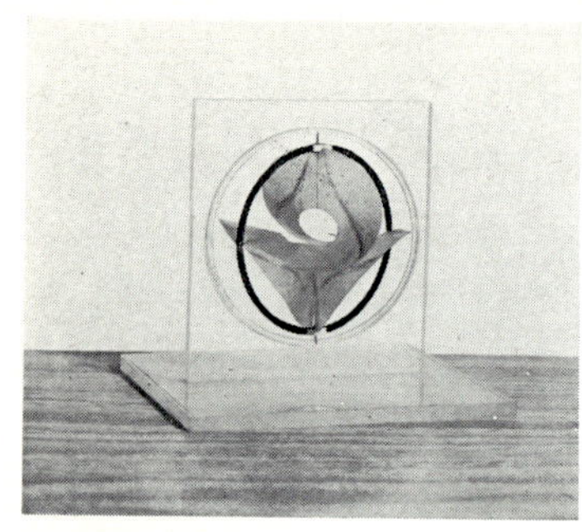

Left
53 Model for 'Spheric Theme' (rotating) c.1937

Below
55 Spheric Theme (penetrated) c.1937

Right
56 Spheric Theme 1960

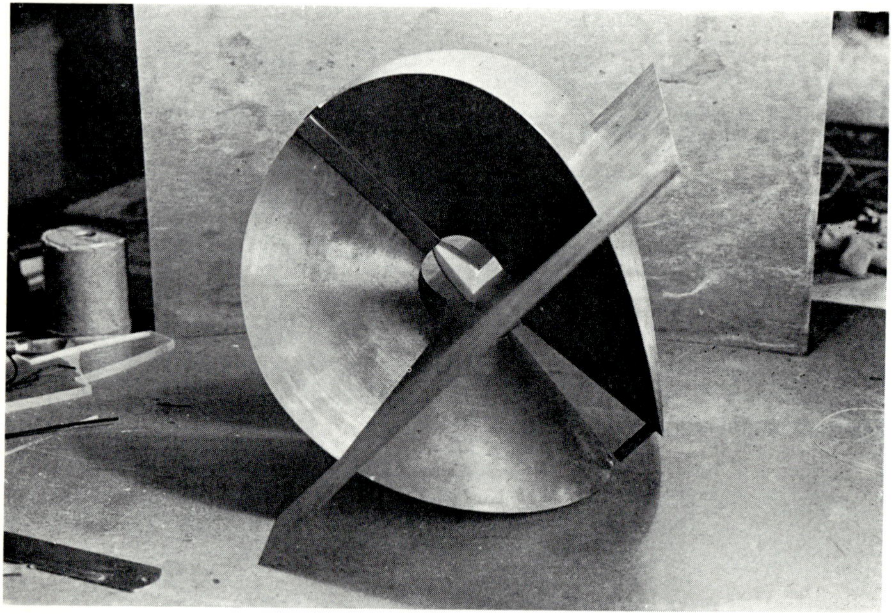

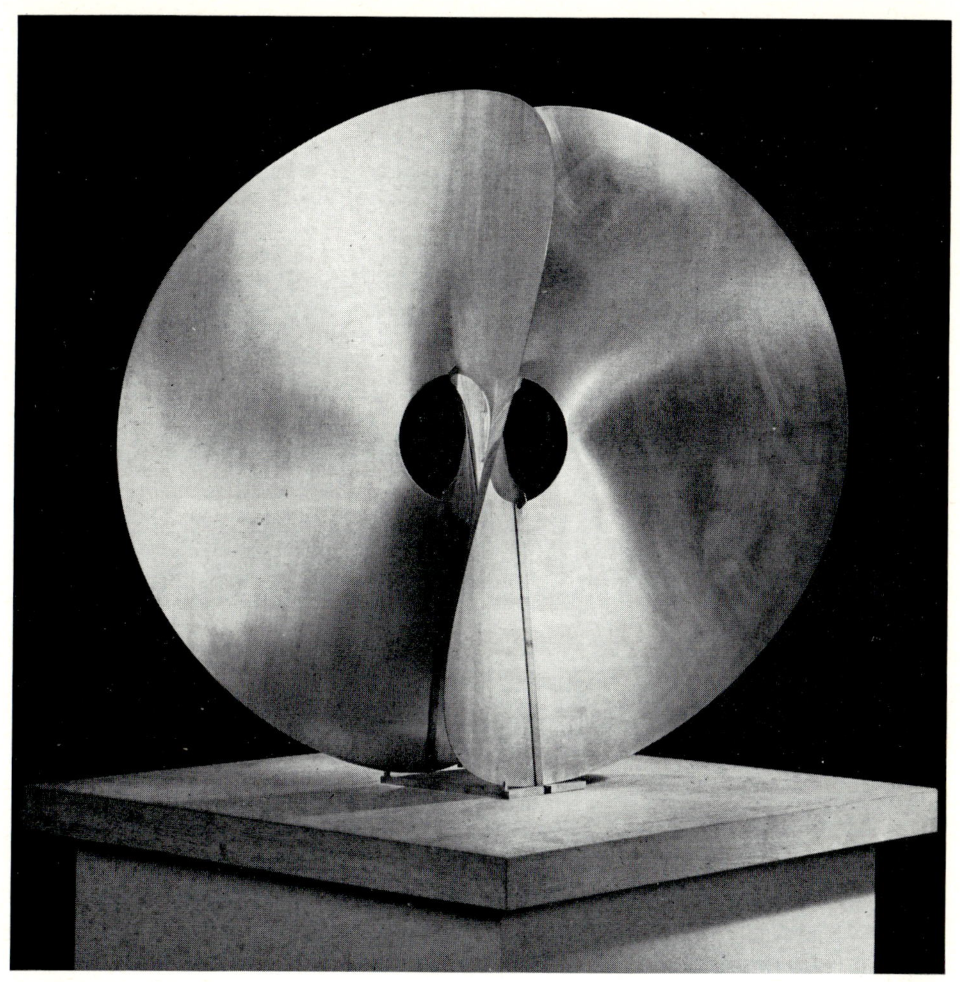

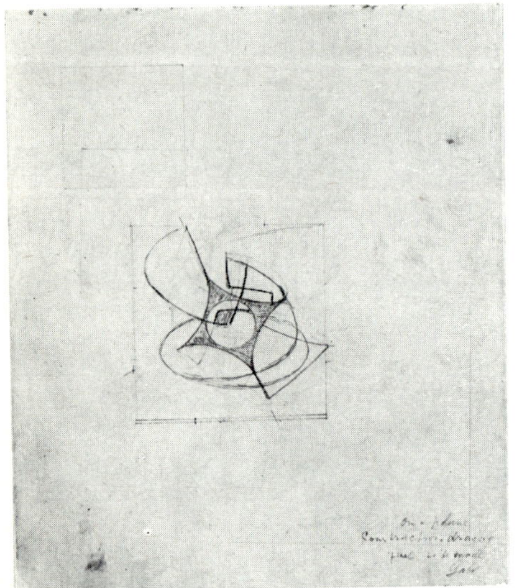

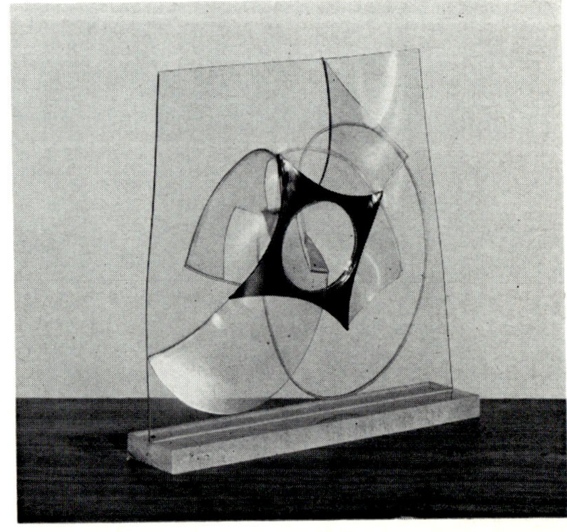

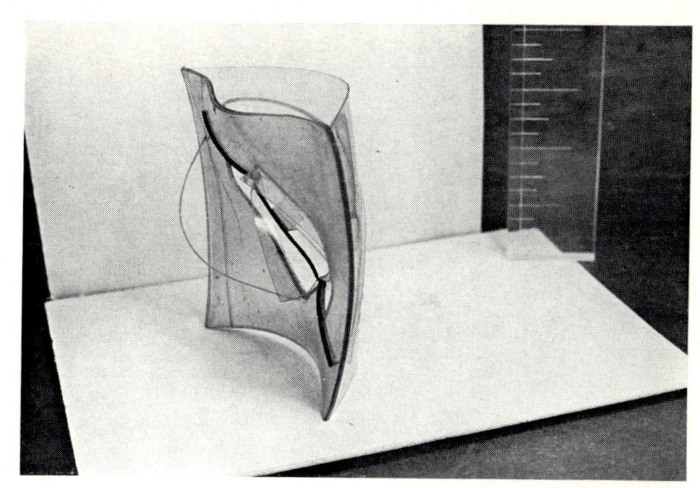

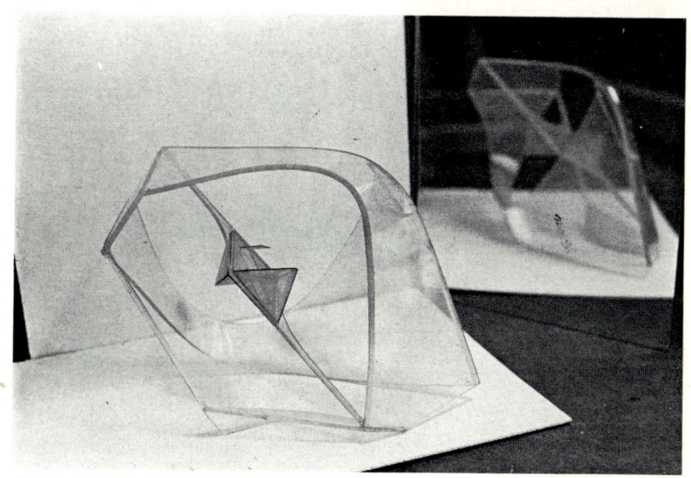

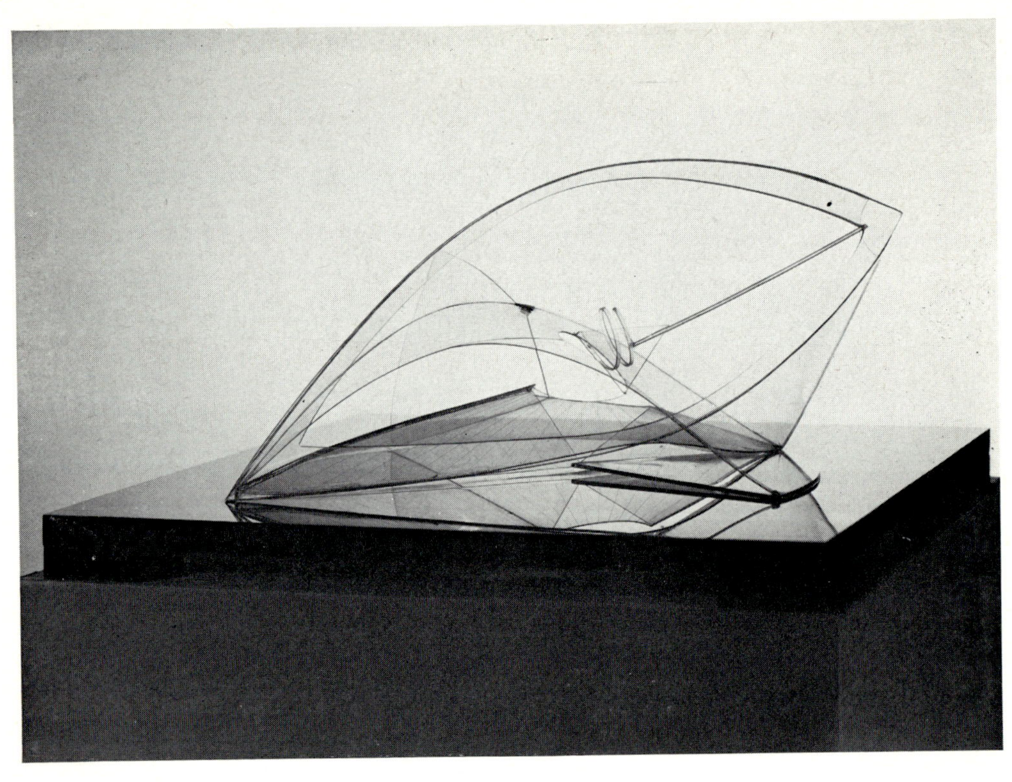

Above
69 Spiral Theme 1941

Right
71 Linear Construction No.1 (variation) 1942–3

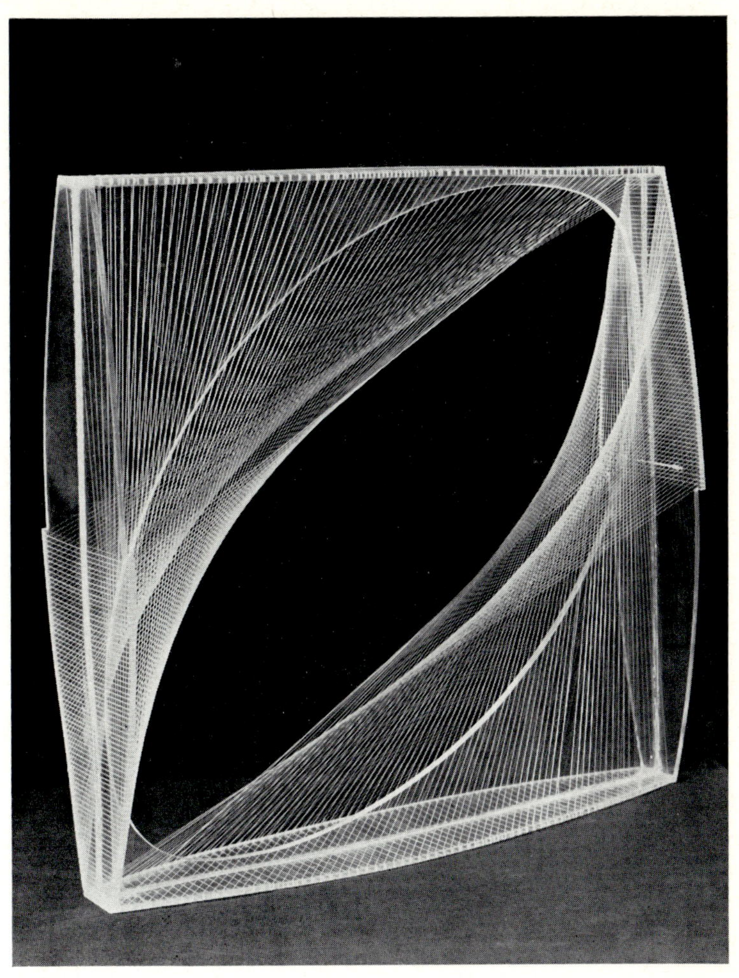

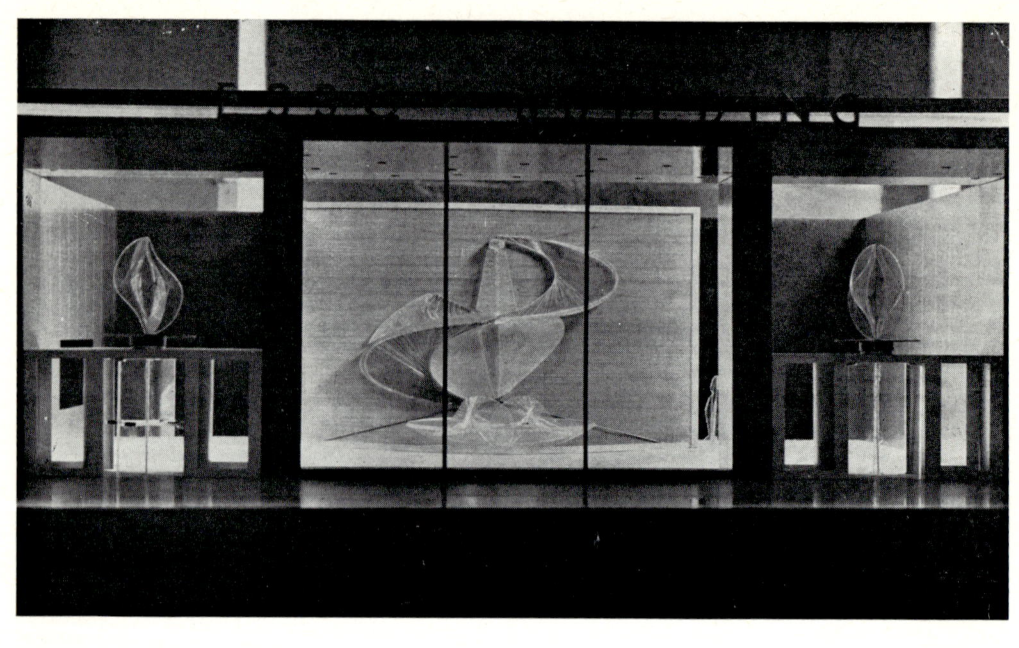

Above
78 Models for Esso project, New York 1949–52

Right
86 Linear Construction No.2
1968–9

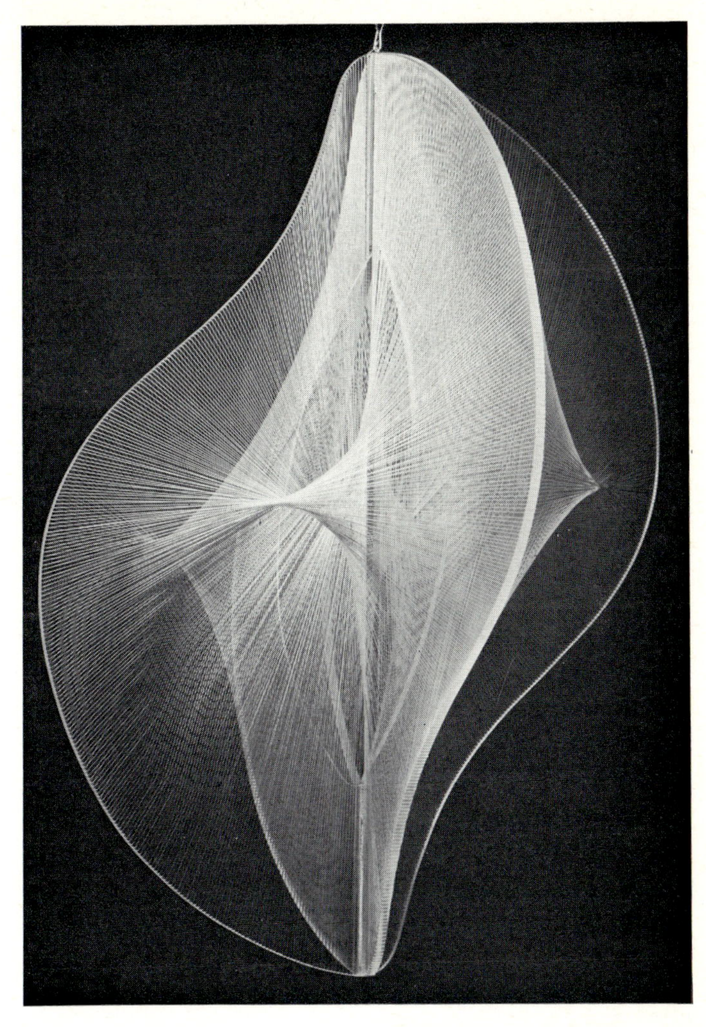

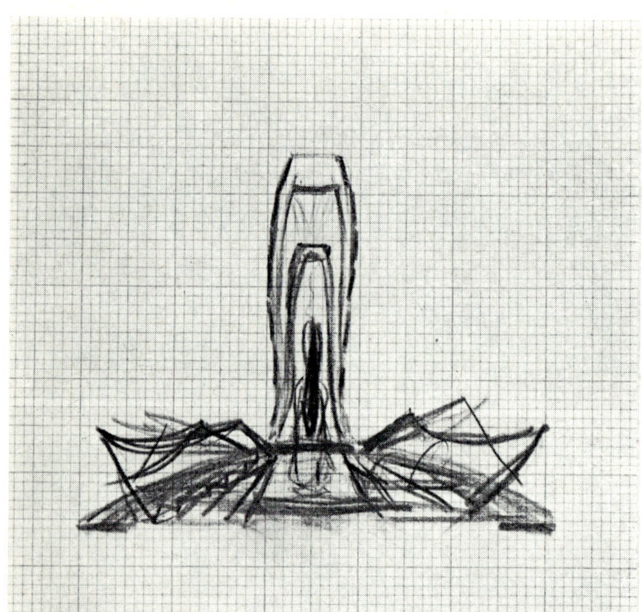

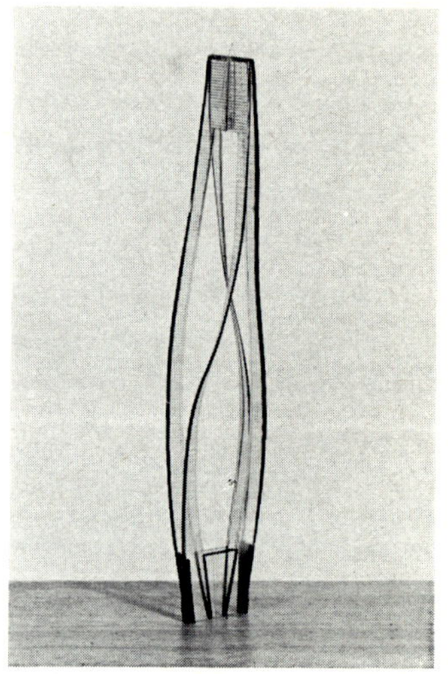

Left
83 Sketch for a construction 1954

Above
84 Model for Bijenkorf c.1954

44

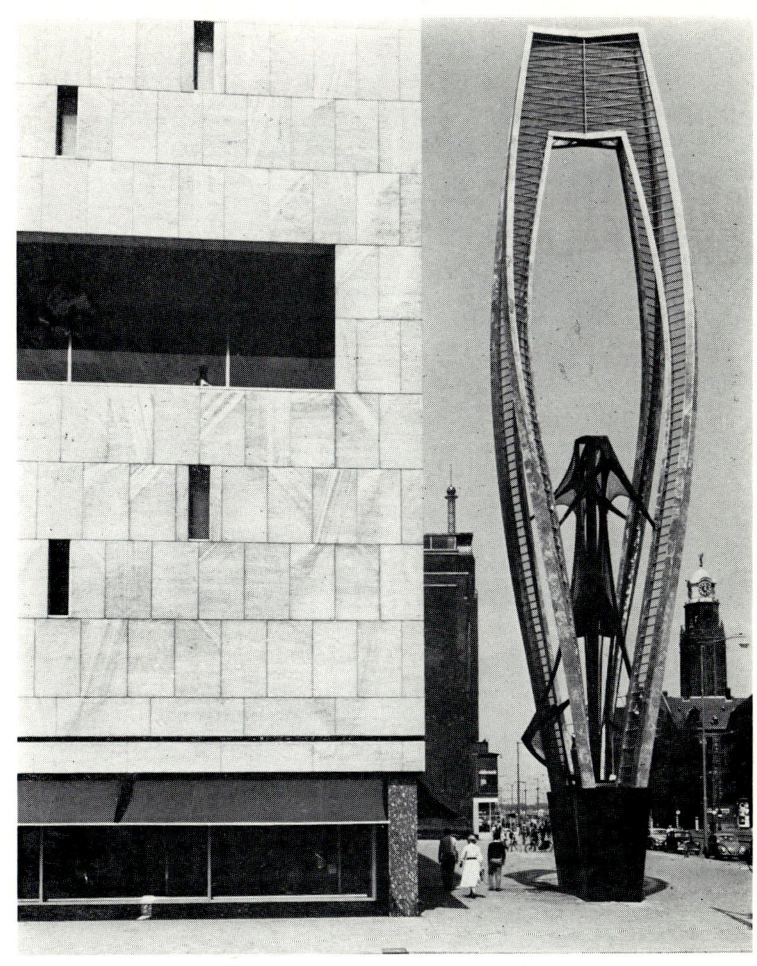

85 Bijenkorf Construction,
Rotterdam 1957

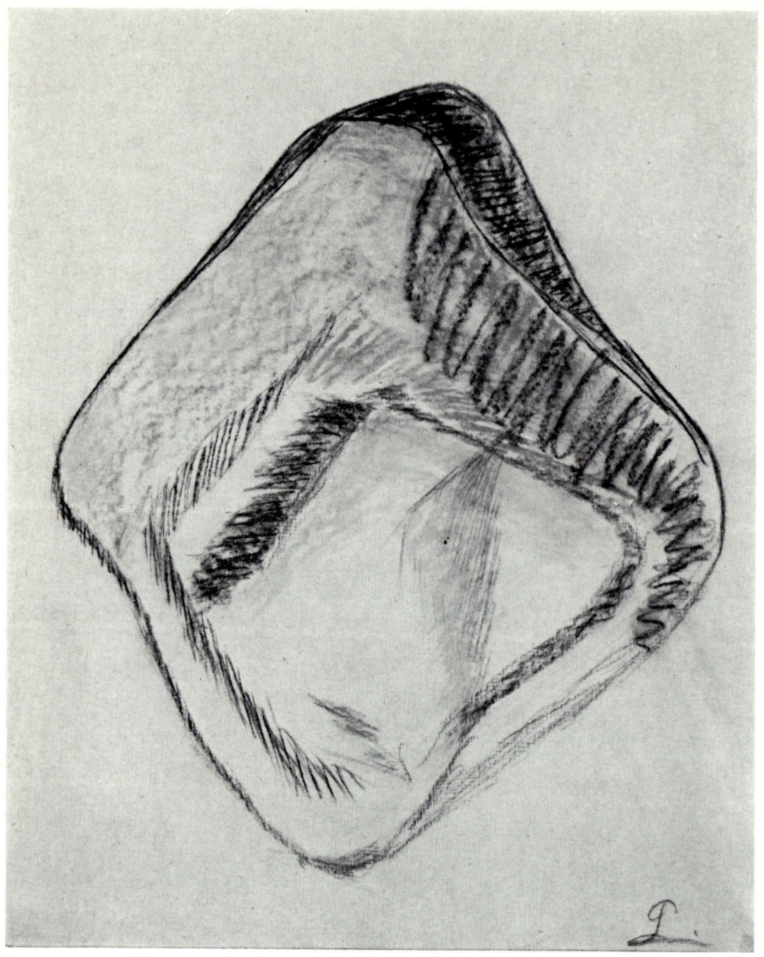

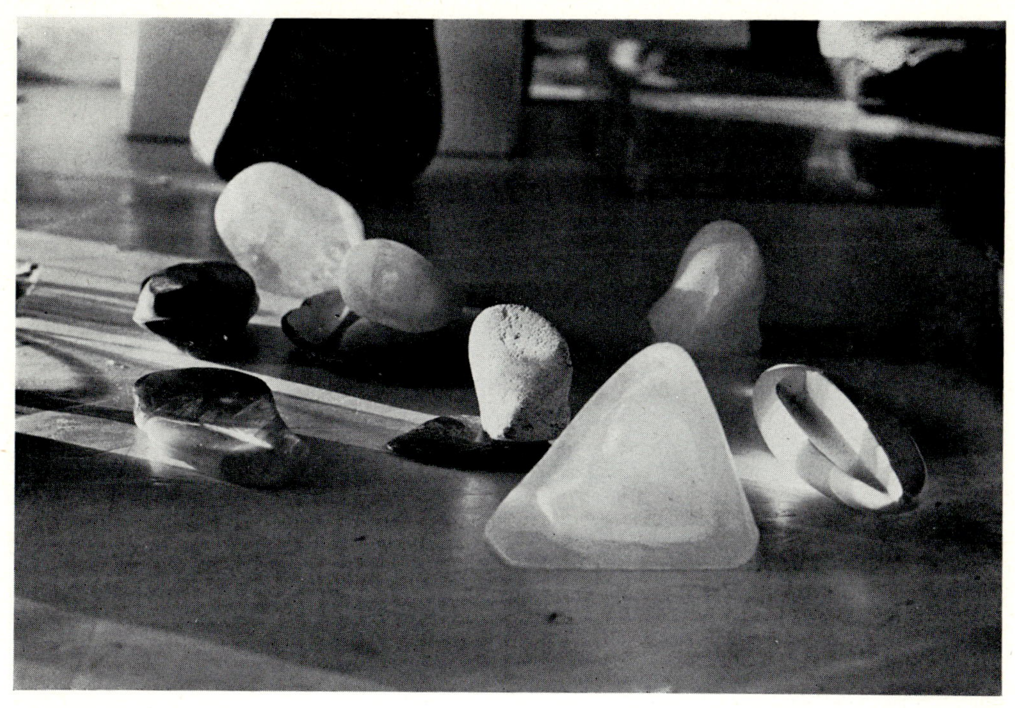

Left
96 Untitled c.1961

Above
Group of miniature stone carvings 1960–70

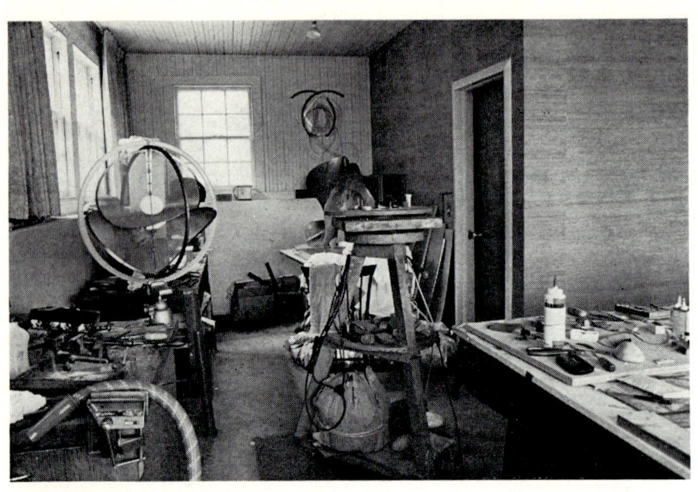

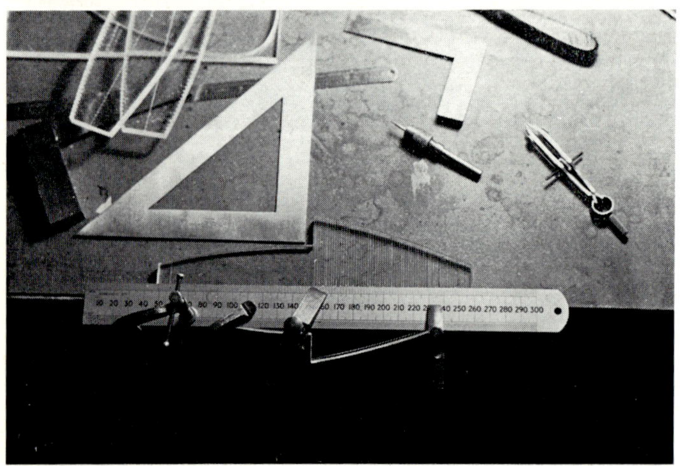

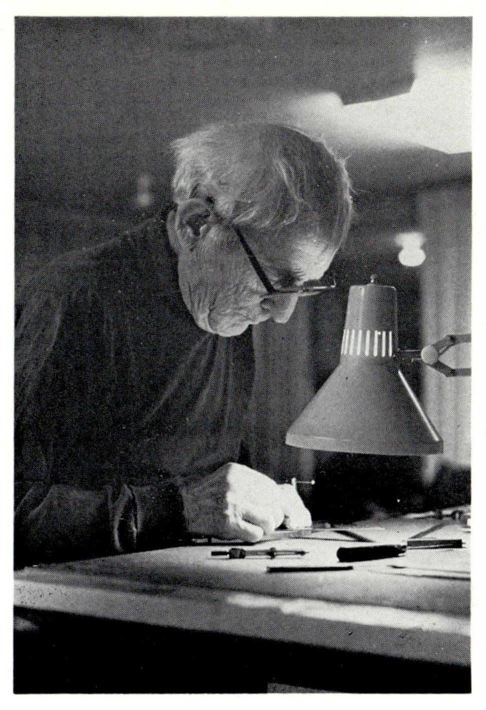

Left
The artist's studio and a selection
of his tools

Above
The artist at work, 1976

Biographical Notes & Principal Exhibitions

1890 Born Briansk, Russia. Named Naum Neemia Pevsner. He had four brothers, including Alexei and Antoine, and one sister.

1910 Graduated from Gymnasium at Kursk. Enrolled in medical faculty at University of Munich.

1910–14 In Munich.

1911 Transferred to study of natural sciences.

1912 Studied engineering at polytechnium school, Munich. During these years attended Professor Wölfflin's lectures on the History of Art. First visit to Paris.

1913 Walking tour through Italy from Munich to Florence and Venice.

1913–14 Visited brother Antoine who was painting in Paris.

1914 At outbreak of war went to Copenhagen, Stockholm and then Oslo with younger brother Alexei.

1915 Made first constructions using the name Gabo. December: joined by elder brother Antoine.

1917 April: returned to Russia.

1919–20 Project for a radio station at Serpuchov.

1920 First public exhibition in the open air on Tverskoi Boulevard, Moscow.
Wrote Realistic Manifesto, published in Moscow, with brother Antoine.
First constructions with motor.

1922–32 Lived in Berlin.

1922 Left Moscow for Berlin. Exhibited in the *Erste Russische Kunstaustellung*, organized by the Soviet Government at the Galerie van Diemen, Berlin.
'Project for a Monument for an Observatory'.

1924 Exhibited at the Galerie Percier, Paris: *Constructivistes Russes: Gabo et Pevsner*.

1924–25 'Project for a Monument for an Airport'.

1925 Project for a monument for the Institute of Physics and Mathematics.

1926 Exhibited for the first time in America at the Little Review Gallery, New York, with Van Doesburg and Pevsner.
Designed set, properties and costumes for Diaghilev's ballet *La Chatte* first performed in Monte Carlo in 1927. Pevsner designed the statue of the goddess.

1929 Project for a *Fete Lumière* for the Brandenburg Gate, Berlin.

1930 First one-man exhibition of constructions at the Kestner-Gesellschaft, Hanover.

1931 Project for the Palace of the Soviets.

1932 Left Germany for Paris.
'Project for a Monument for an Airport'.

1932–35   Member of the group *Abstraction-Création*.

1935   First visit to England.

1936   Exhibited with fifteen artists in *Abstract and Concrete* at the Lefèvre
       Gallery, London.
       Exhibited with Pevsner at the Chicago Arts Club. Seven works in-
       cluded in *Cubism and Abstract Art* at the Museum of Modern Art, New
       York.
       Married Miriam Israels in London.

1937   Edited with J. L. Martin and Ben Nicholson *Circle: International Survey
       of Constructive Art*.
       Two works included in large Constructivist exhibition at the Kunst-
       halle, Basel, and two in Constructivist exhibition at the London
       Gallery, London.

1938   One-man exhibition at the London Gallery, London.
       Visited the United States: exhibited at the Wadsworth Atheneum,
       Hartford, at the Julien Levy Gallery, New York and at Vassar College,
       Poughkeepsie. *Spheric theme* purchased as a fountain project for the
       General Electric Company pavilion at the New York World's Fair,
       but never installed.

1939   At outbreak of war moved to Carbis Bay, Cornwall. Exhibited one
       work in the San Francisco Golden Gate exhibition in section 'Sculp-
       ture in Setting'.

1941   Birth of daughter Nina-Serafina.

1942   Exhibited in *New Movements in Art. Contemporary Work in England*,
       London Museum, London.

1944   Member of Design Research Unit, London.
       Produced an advanced design for a car for Jowett which did not go
       into production.

1946 Left England for the United States.

1948 Exhibited with Pevsner at the Museum of Modern Art, New York.

1950 Commissioned to make construction for the Sadie A. May wing of the
      Baltimore Museum of Art.

1951 Baltimore construction completed and installed.
      Exhibition at the Massachusetts Institute of Technology.

1952 Became citizen of United States of America.
      Exhibition, with Josef Albers, at the Chicago Arts Club.

1953 One-man exhibition at the Pierre Matisse Gallery, New York. Exhi-
      bition, with Alexander Calder, at the Wadsworth Atheneum,
      Hartford. Awarded second prize in the *Unknown Political Prisoner.*
      international sculpture competition.

1953–54 Professor at Harvard University Graduate School of Architecture.

1954 Awarded Guggenheim Fellowship. Awarded Mr. and Mrs. Frank G.
      Logan Medal of the Art Institute of Chicago.

1955 Commissioned to make sculpture for the Bijenkorf Building in
      Rotterdam.

1956 Commissioned by Wallace K. Harrison to make bas-relief for the
      U.S. Rubber Company, Rockefeller Centre, New York. Completed
      in November.

1957 Bijenkorf construction completed and installed.

1960 Prize from Brandeis University.

1962 June: Visited brothers Mark, Jeremy and Alexei in Moscow and
      Leningrad.

1965   Elected member of the Institute of the American Academy of Art and Letters.

1965–66   Retrospective exhibition at the Stedelijk Museum, Amsterdam; the Kunsthalle, Mannheim; the Wilhelm-Lehmbruck-Museum, Duisburg; the Kunsthaus, Zurich; the Moderna Museet, Stockholm; the Tate Gallery, London.

1967   Awarded Honorary Doctorate at Royal College of Art, London.

1970   Commissioned to make fountain, installed at St. Thomas's Hospital in 1975.

1971   Awarded the Hon. K.B.E.

1970–72   Travelling Exhibition: Louisiana, Humblebaeck; Oslo, Nasjonal galeriet; Berlin, Nationalgalerie; Hanover, Kunstverein; Grenoble, Musée de Peinture et de Sculpture; Paris, Museé National d'Art Moderne; Lisbon, Gulbenkian Foundation.

1973   Commissioned to make sculpture for the Nationalgalerie, Berlin.

Lives in Middlebury, Connecticut.

Catalogue

Dimensions are given in inches and centimetres, in the order: height, width, depth. All works belong to the artist and his family unless otherwise stated.

1 **Head No.2** (enlarged version, 1964, of 1916 original)
Iron, $69 \times 52\frac{3}{4} \times 48 / 175.3 \times 136.5 \times 121.9$
Tate Gallery (T.1520)

2 **Christmas** 1910
Pastel, $14\frac{1}{2} \times 17\frac{3}{4} / 37 \times 45$

3 **Drawing for a constructed head** 1916
Pencil, $7\frac{1}{2} \times 6\frac{3}{4} / 19 \times 17.2$

4 **Head No.2** 1916
Steel, $17\frac{3}{4} \times 16 \times 16 / 45 \times 40.5 \times 40.5$

5 **Two Cubes (demonstrating stereometric method)**
Plywood, each $12 \times 12 \times 12 / 30.5^3$

6 **Sketch** 1917
Pencil, $7\frac{1}{2} \times 5\frac{1}{2} / 19 \times 14$

7 **Sketch** 1917
Pencil, $9\frac{1}{8} \times 9\frac{1}{8} / 23.2 \times 23.2$

8 **Sketch for a relief construction** 1917
Pencil, $7 \times 5 / 17.8 \times 12.7$

9 **Design for a construction in a niche** 1918
Pencil, $9\frac{5}{8} \times 7\frac{5}{8} / 24.5 \times 19.4$
Several of these 'wall' constructions were realized in Russia but have since been lost or destroyed.

10 **Drawing** 1917
Pencil, $9\frac{1}{8} \times 9\frac{1}{8} / 23.2 \times 23.2$

11 **Sketch for a kinetic construction** 1917
Pencil, $6\frac{1}{2} \times 5\frac{3}{4} / 16.5 \times 14.6$

12 **Sketch for a construction** 1918
Pencil, $8 \times 5 / 20.3 \times 12.7$

13 **Kinetic Sculpture (Standing Wave)** 1920
Metal, $24\frac{1}{2} \times 9\frac{1}{2} \times 7\frac{1}{2} / 62.2 \times 24.1 \times 19$
Tate Gallery (T.827)

14 **Sketch for a kinetic construction** 1922
Crayon on graph paper, $3\frac{3}{4} \times 6\frac{1}{2} / 9.5 \times 16.5$

15 **Sketch for a mobile construction** c. 1918
Pencil, $11\frac{1}{2} \times 9\frac{1}{2} / 29.2 \times 24.1$

16 **Sketch for a Monument for an Institute of Physics and Mathematics** 1919
Pencil, $11 \times 8 / 28 \times 20.3$
This project was realized in 1925. The finished construction, 24 in / 61 cm high in glass and metal, is in the U.S.S.R.

17 **Model for 'Column'** 1923
Plastic, $5\frac{1}{2} \times 2\frac{1}{4} \times 2\frac{1}{4}/14 \times 5.7 \times 5.7$

18 **Column** 1923
Plastic, $10 \times 4\frac{1}{2} \times 4\frac{1}{2}/25.4 \times 11.5 \times 11.5$
Nina S. Gabo

19 **Column** (enlarged version 1975 of 1923 original)
Stainless steel, glass and perspex, $76\frac{3}{8} \times 60\frac{5}{8}/$
194×154 diameter
This design represents the culmination of Gabo's
'Column' series of 1922–3.

20 **Sketch** 1918–19
Pencil, $9\frac{1}{2} \times 8\frac{1}{2}/24.1 \times 21.6$

21 **Model for Monument for an Airport** 1923
Plastic, $2\frac{1}{2} \times 4\frac{3}{4} \times 3/6.3 \times 12 \times 7.6$
This is a variation on Gabo's first project for an
airport 1924–5.

22 **Circular Relief** 1925
Plastic on wooden base, $19\frac{1}{2}/49.5$ diameter

23 **Model for 'Construction in Space
"2 Cones"'** 1927
Plastic, $3\frac{3}{8} \times 4\frac{1}{4} \times 4\frac{7}{8}/8.3 \times 10.8 \times 12.4$

24 **Construction in Space, '2 Cones'** 1927
Plastic on wooden base, $24 \times 24/61 \times 61$

25 **Model for 'Double Relief in a Niche'**
c.1929
Plastic, cork and cardboard, $4\frac{1}{2} \times 8\frac{3}{4} \times 2/$
$11.4 \times 22.2 \times 5.1$
This relief construction was designed for the architect Eric Mendelsohn's apartment in Dahlem but
the commission was abandoned and Gabo developed
his idea in the two following constructions.

26 **Red Cavern** 1928–9
Plastic, metals and cork set into wooden boxes,
$25\frac{3}{8} \times 20\frac{3}{8}/64.5 \times 51.7$

27 **In a Niche** 1928–9
Plastic, metals and cork set into wooden boxes,
$25\frac{3}{8} \times 20\frac{3}{8}/64.5 \times 51.7$

28 **Costume sketch for the ballet 'La Chatte'** 1926
Pencil on graph paper, $10 \times 7\frac{1}{2}/25.4 \times 19$

29 **Costume sketch for the ballet 'La Chatte'** 1926
Pastel, $11 \times 9/28 \times 22.9$

30 **Costume sketch for the ballet 'La Chatte'** 1926
Pastel, $11 \times 9/28 \times 22.9$

31 **Two photographs of revolving set for 'La
Chatte'** 1926
These photographs are all that remain of the ori-
ginal set.

32 **Sketch 'Monte Carlo'** 1926
Pencil and crayon, $10\frac{1}{2} \times 8/26.7 \times 20.3$

33 **Photograph of project for a Fête Lumière** 1929
The photograph shows the design only; the work
was not realized.

Torsion Theme 1929–73

34 **Model for 'Torsion'** 1929
Plastic, $3\frac{1}{2} \times 3\frac{3}{4} \times 3\frac{3}{4}/8.9 \times 9.5 \times 9.5$

35 **Torsion** 1929
Plastic, $13\frac{3}{4}/34.9$

36 **Torsion (project for a fountain)** 1960–4
Bronze, $30 \times 33\frac{1}{8} \times 33\frac{1}{8}/76.2 \times 84.1 \times 84.1$
Tate Gallery (T.1171)

37 **Photograph of 'Torsion Fountain'**
1972–3
Aluminium, 122 × 132 × 132/
309.8 × 335.3 × 335.3
Installed in front of St. Thomas's Hospital, London,
1975.

38 **Sketch for a carving in stone** 1930
Crayon and gouache, $10\frac{3}{4} \times 13\frac{1}{4}$/27.3 × 33.7

39 **Sketch for a stone carving** 1933
Pencil and crayon, $6\frac{1}{2} \times 6$/16.5 × 15.2

40 **Sketch for a stone carving** 1933
Pencil, $5\frac{1}{8} \times 8\frac{5}{8}$/13 × 22

41 **Sketch** c.1933
Pencil on squared paper, $4\frac{3}{4} \times 8\frac{1}{4}$/12 × 21

42 **Sketch for 'The Urn'** c.1933
Pencil, $10\frac{7}{8} \times 8$/27.6 × 20.3

43 **Model for 'Stone with a Collar'** 1930–31
Portland stone on slate, $2 \times 2 \times 1\frac{1}{4}$/5 × 5 × 3.1

44 **Stone with Collar** 1930–1
Portland stone on slate, $7 \times 6 \times 3\frac{1}{8}$/
17.8 × 15.2 × 8

45 **Quartz Stone Carving** 1936–40
White quartz, $6\frac{1}{2} \times 10\frac{1}{4} \times 8$/16.5 × 26 × 20.3

46 **Untitled** 1939
Oil on paper, $5\frac{5}{8} \times 5\frac{7}{8}$/14.3 × 14.9

47 **Granite Carving** c.1940
Tintagel stone, $4\frac{3}{4} \times 5\frac{3}{4}$/12 × 14.6

Spheric Theme 1935–60

48 **Sketch for 'Spheric Theme'** 1935–7
Blue crayon, $7\frac{3}{4} \times 12\frac{3}{4}$/19.7 × 32.4

49 **Sketch for 'Spheric Theme'** 1935
Pen, $9\frac{1}{2} \times 8$/24.1 × 20.3

50 **Model for 'Spheric Theme'** c.1937
Opaque plastic, $4\frac{3}{4} \times 3\frac{5}{8} \times 3\frac{1}{2}$/12.1 × 9.2 × 8.9

51 **Model for 'Spheric Theme'** c.1937
Metal, $4 \times 3 \times 3\frac{1}{4}$/10.2 × 7.6 × 8.2

52 **Model for 'Spheric Theme'** c.1937
Plastic, $3\frac{1}{4} \times 4 \times 3\frac{1}{4}$/8.2 × 10.2 × 8.2

53 **Model for 'Spheric Theme' (rotating
version)** c.1937
Plastic, plastic coated paper, pencil,
$3\frac{1}{2} \times 3 \times 2\frac{1}{4}$/8.9 × 7.6 × 5.7

54 **Spheric Theme (variation)** c.1937
Bronze, $6 \times 4\frac{5}{8} \times 4\frac{1}{2}$/15.2 × 11.7 × 11.4
Private Collection

55 **Spheric Theme (penetrated variation)** c.1937
Bronze, 13 × 13 × 13/33 × 33 × 33

56 **Spheric Theme** (enlarged version 1960 of c.1937
original)
Bronze with bronze springs, motorized version,
$36\frac{1}{4} \times 26\frac{1}{4} \times 28\frac{1}{2}$/92 × 66.8 × 72.4
Tate Gallery (T.826)
In a more recent variation (1974) of 'Spheric Theme'
the bronze surface is enriched by stretched springs.

57 **Sketch for 'Construction on a Plane'** c.1935–7
Pencil, $9 \times 7\frac{3}{4}$/22.8 × 19.7

58 **Model for 'Construction on a Plane'** c.1935–7
Plastic, $6 \times 6 \times 1\frac{1}{4}/15.2 \times 15.2 \times 3.1$

59 **Construction on a Plane** 1935–7
Plastic, $19 \times 19 \times 8\frac{1}{2}/48.2 \times 48.2 \times 21.6$
Private collection
This version, with black centre, is a variation on the
original plastic construction. There is a further
variation with a white centre.

60 **Model for 'Construction on a Line'** 1935–7
Plastic, $4\frac{1}{4} \times 4 \times 1\frac{1}{2}/10.8 \times 10.1 \times 3.8$

61 **Construction on a Line** 1937
Plastic, $18 \times 17/45.7 \times 43.2$
Mrs Lois Ventris
This work was made in memory of Michael Ventris,
who deciphered the Linear B Script of Ancient
Crete.

62 **Model for 'Construction in Space' 'Crystal'**
1937
Plastic, $3 \times 3 \times 1\frac{1}{2}/7.6 \times 7.6 \times 3.8$

63 **Model for 'Construction in Space with
Crystalline Centre'** 1938
Plastic, $4 \times 6\frac{1}{8} \times 2\frac{3}{4}/10.1 \times 15.6 \times 7$

64 **The Green Bowl** 1939
Pastel, $10 \times 12\frac{3}{4}/25.4 \times 32.3$

65 **Sketch** 1940
Pencil and wash, $11\frac{1}{2} \times 12\frac{1}{2}/29.2 \times 31.8$

66 **Untitled** 1941
Pencil and watercolour, $7\frac{1}{2} \times 7\frac{1}{2}/19 \times 19$
Private collection

67 **Sketch** 1941
Gouache, $10\frac{1}{4} \times 13\frac{3}{4}/26 \times 34.9$

68 **Model for 'Spiral Theme'** 1941
Plastic, $2\frac{1}{2} \times 6\frac{3}{4} \times 4\frac{1}{2}/6.3 \times 17.2 \times 11.4$

69 **Spiral Theme** 1941
Plastic, $5\frac{1}{2} \times 9\frac{5}{8} \times 9\frac{5}{8}/14 \times 24.4 \times 24.4$
Tate Gallery (T.190)

70 **Model for 'Linear Construction No.1'**
1942–3
Plastic with nylon strings,
$4 \times 4 \times 1/10.1 \times 10.1 \times 2.5$
Nina S. Gabo

71 **Linear Construction No.1 (variation)** 1942–3
Plastic with nylon strings,
$13\frac{7}{8} \times 13\frac{1}{2} \times 3\frac{1}{2}/35.2 \times 34.3 \times 8.8$
Tate Gallery (T.191)
The Tate Gallery's version with stepped sides is the
earlier of two more elaborate variations on the
theme of the model.

72 **Sketch for a sculpture** 1950
Pencil, $13\frac{1}{2} \times 10\frac{1}{2}/34.3 \times 26.7$

73 **Sketch for a kinetic construction** 1921
Pencil on graph paper, $11\frac{7}{8} \times 9/30.1 \times 22.8$

74 **Model for (lower section of) Baltimore
Construction** 1950–1
Plastic, $8\frac{1}{2} \times 2 \times 2/21.5 \times 5.1 \times 5.1$

75 **Photograph of installation at Baltimore
Museum of Art** 1951
Aluminium, phosphor bronze, plastic, stainless
steel and rolled gold wire, 15 ft. high approx.

76 **Model for 'Shadow Piece'** 1951–2
Bronze construction with pencil drawing on
manuscript paper,
$4\frac{1}{4} \times 8\frac{3}{4} \times 2\frac{1}{4}/10.8 \times 22.2 \times 5.7$

77 **Model for the Esso project, Radio City,
New York** 1949–52
Plastic and gold wire mesh,
$3\frac{1}{2} \times 5 \times 2/8.9 \times 12.7 \times 5$
This construction was designed for the 51st Street
entrance of the Esso Building.

78 **Photograph of models showing triple
scheme for the 51st Street entrance lobby**
These models, now in the Museum of Modern
Art, New York, include (left and right above the
doors) early versions of 'Linear Construction No.2'.

79 **Model for 'Linear Construction No.3 with
Red'** 1953
Plastic and nylon thread,
$3\frac{3}{4} \times 2\frac{1}{4} \times 2\frac{3}{8}/9.5 \times 5.7 \times 6$
This has been realized in large-scale versions.

80 **Photograph of bas relief made for U.S. Rubber
Company Building, New York City** 1956
Aluminium, phosphor bronze, plastic, 10 ft.
diameter
This construction, now re-sited at the Celanese
Building, Avenue of the Americas, New York, in-
corporates a version of 'Linear Construction No.3
with Red'.

81 **First model for a 'Monument to the
Unknown Political Prisoner'** 1953
Plastic and wire mesh,
$5 \times 1\frac{1}{4} \times 1/12.7 \times 3.1 \times 2.5$

82 **Model for a 'Monument to the Unknown
Political Prisoner'** 1953
Plastic and wire mesh, $15\frac{1}{2} \times 3\frac{1}{2}/39.4 \times 8.9$
Gabo was awarded 2nd prize for his design in this
international competition. The model was not
enlarged further.

83 **Sketch for a construction** 1954
Pencil on graph paper, $9\frac{1}{4} \times 7\frac{1}{2}/23.5 \times 19$

84 **Model for a construction at the Bijenkorf
Building, Rotterdam** 1954–7
Plastic, $9\frac{7}{8} \times 1\frac{3}{4} \times 1\frac{3}{4}/25.1 \times 4.4 \times 4.4$

85 **Photograph of the Bijenkorf Construction
on site** completed 1957
Pre-stressed concrete, steel ribs, stainless steel,
bronze wires and marble, height 80 ft.

86 **Linear Construction No.2** 1968–9
Nylon thread and plastic,
$45\frac{1}{4} \times 32\frac{7}{8} \times 32\frac{7}{8}/114.9 \times 83.5 \times 83.5$
Tate Gallery (T.1105)
This work relates to the models made for the
Esso project (see No.78). This enlarged version of
'Linear Construction No.2', 1949–52, was presented
to the Tate Gallery by Gabo in memory of Sir
Herbert Read. The work exists in several versions.

87 **Three untitled models (variations on a
theme)** c.1953
Plastic with metal wires, each approx.
$3 \times 1\frac{1}{2} \times 1\frac{1}{2}/7.6 \times 3.8 \times 3.8$

88 **Model for a hanging construction** c.1955
Plastic, $7\frac{3}{4}/9.7$

89 **Model for hanging piece** c.1957
Plastic, $6 \times 3\frac{1}{4} \times 1\frac{1}{2}/15.2 \times 8.2 \times 3.8$

90 **Model for 'Vertical Construction No.1'**
1964–5
Bronze with steel strings,
$4\frac{5}{8} \times 1\frac{3}{8} \times 1\frac{3}{8}/11.7 \times 3.5 \times 3.5$
This has been realized in several versions, some of
which are motorized.

91 (Section of) model for 'Construction in
Space, Suspended' 1965
Plastic and nylon thread, $4\frac{1}{4} \times 4\frac{1}{4}$ / 10.8 × 10.8

92 Construction in Space, Suspended 1965
Bronze, aluminium, plastic and nylon,
12 × 11 × 11 / 30.5 × 28 × 28
Nina S. Gabo
The enlarged version of this work is $22\frac{1}{2}$ in high.

93 Ten miniature carvings 1960–70
Various stones, alabaster and plaster

94 Polished stone carving
$6\frac{1}{4} \times 5\frac{1}{2}$ / 15.9 × 14

Untitled Drawings and Sketches c.1950–65

95 Untitled c.1953–60
Pencil, $9\frac{1}{2} \times 7\frac{3}{4}$ / 24.1 × 19.7

96 Untitled c.1961
Coloured crayon on tissue paper,
$21\frac{1}{2} \times 17\frac{1}{2}$ / 54.6 × 44.5

97 Untitled 1961
Pencil, oil and gouache, $14\frac{1}{2} \times 10\frac{3}{4}$ / 36.2 × 27.3

98 Untitled sketch c.1960
Oil on paper, $7\frac{1}{4} \times 6\frac{1}{2}$ / 18.4 × 16.5

99 Space c.1970
Oil on board, $21\frac{1}{2}$ / 54.6 diameter

Bibliography

Selected Writings by the artist

'The Constructive Idea in Art', *Circle*, International Survey of Constructive Art, London 1937.

'Sculpture: Carving and Construction in Space', *Circle*, International Survey of Constructive Art, London 1937.

'Of Divers Arts', lectures given at the National Gallery of Art, Washington in 1959, pub. Pantheon Books, New York 1962.

Selected Writings on the artist

Read, Herbert and Martin, Leslie, *Gabo*, Lund Humphries, London 1957.

Pevsner, Alexei, *A biographical sketch of my brothers: Naum Gabo and Antoine Pevsner*, Augustin and Schoonman, Amsterdam 1964.

'Naum Gabo and the Constructivist Tradition', special issue, *Studio International*, London April 1966.

Rickey, George, *Constructivism, Origins and Evolution*, G. Braziller, New York 1967.